TESTIMONIALS FOR RED, WHITE AND BLUES

"Linda's courage to write about her painful trauma is an inspiration for the many Native women who suffered the same fate as children and young women. Her story is one of abuse, secrets, anger, revelation, and a lifetime journey to heal her soul."

> Doreen Blaker
> Baraga, MI

"It made me laugh, it made me cry. It made me feel good and comforted knowing someone who went through the same things as me could overcome them, make peace with it all, be successful, and have a wonderful life."

> Danielle Madosh
> Palmer, MI

"I really enjoyed reading, *Red, White & Blues*. I have lived here all of my life. I would have never known the adversity that she and the people around her went through. The book is a very heartfelt story of a generation, like mine, but how different our childhoods were. Once I started reading, I could not put it down."

> Jenelle Ninko
> Conover, WI

"A heartbreakingly great read that lets you see the soul and strength of a woman who has withstood the ugliest side of society. Linda's survival and triumph demonstrate an incredible resolve and will serve as an inspiration to many."

> Pat Garrison
> Eagle River, WI

"From the moment I picked up the book, *Red, White & Blues*, by Linda Raye Cobe, I was gripped with interest. The way she was able to express her feelings and tell of the horrible life experiences she had growing up, kept me from putting the book down. Throughout the entire story, Linda has shown that she is a survivor and I give her much credit for the way she has been able to share that with others."

> Ronald T. Pongracz
> Rexton, MI

RED, WHITE & BLUES

By Linda Raye Cobe

Publisher's Cataloging-in-Publication Data
Cobe, Linda Raye
Red, white & blues/Linda Cobe
Naubinway, Mich.

ISBN 978-1-4951-5872-8

Cover photography by Tom Vranich

Book production by Bookability of Michigan LLC

Printed in the United States of America

Acknowledgements and Dedication

I wish to thank my husband, Randy, first and foremost, for believing in me and supporting my writing endeavor. His patience and understanding have given me the gentle nudge that I needed to follow my desire.

My biggest sense of inspiration and encouragement has came from Jeannie Ballew, a newly found friend, neighbor, retired teacher, writer, and poet. Jeannie has painstakingly assisted me with the editing of this book. Her insight and recommendations have enhanced my final work. Without her guidance, this project may not have reached completion.

I also want to thank Tom Vranich who provided the technical support needed to get my book to publication. His knowledge, experience, and professionalism eased the path and provided the direction I was looking for.

To my sister, thank you for being part of my story and part of my life. To other friends and relatives who wished me well and believed in me, thank you also.

I also thank my brother-in-law, Will, who provided me with his computer expertise in the development of this book.

This book is dedicated to my four children, Jeremiah, Zachery, Rachel, and Adam, whom I love with every ounce of energy in me. I hope it gives them a better understanding of their mother, their ancestry, and enriches their appreciation toward life.

Contents

Preface

I've always loved to write from the time I first held a pencil in my hand and was taught the alphabet. My artistic genes came out as I learned to write in cursive. I imitated the letters and made them look exactly as I saw them on the charts of the schoolroom. As I got older, I realized that the correct words were the tools to effective communication and understanding.

My thoughts and feelings seemed to flow more easily on paper, although my limited vocabulary made me struggle as I searched to express what was deep in my heart. I felt that if people understood me then they couldn't help but love me. And love was the elusive stranger in my desperate search for happiness.

There's something about seeing my own words reflected back at me that helps to confirm my reality. This is a story that may have been told before by others before me. My story comes from a Native American perspective. It is not unique, for what happened to me also happened to so many of our people. In my field of sociology, this is referred to as "actual representation." It is my hope that it will serve as an example of the perseverance and resiliency mustered by our people in the face of great loss.

What shows on the outside isn't necessarily the truth of what is going on inside the heart, mind, and soul of someone. We may give the impression that everything is fine but internally feel like we are dying. So many bad things have happened to me in my lifetime. It was during those dark times that I wondered if such things happened to others also. Was I cursed for a misdeed committed by someone in my family? What could be so wrong with me that people felt they could treat me so badly? I lived in so much pain, but nobody seemed to care. There was no one I trusted enough to reach out to for help.

In my youth I began by writing about that pain. My adopted mother bought me a diary. I journaled from a teenager's point of view with hormones raging. I wrote of the difficulty in dealing with feelings of fear that sometimes became paralyzing. It was hard to enjoy the good times knowing the pain of sadness, disappointment, and heartbreak was just around the corner.

I would write about the things and people that disgusted me. I didn't care to be around the individuals who were fake or users of people. I didn't like to see people picked on just for being different. Things that looked, smelled or sounded gross easily disgusted me. I had a very weak stomach that had me dry heaving or retching, especially if I saw or heard someone else throwing up.

I was just as easily frightened. I wrote about my many fears in life. I was scared of the dark, scared of monsters, bugs, snakes, scared of adults, scared of the unknown, but mostly scared of not being loved.

When I wrote about what was missing in my life, the security of love from parents, siblings, friends, or boyfriends, it would evoke the most painful thoughts and feelings. I would counter that by exploring my ideas of romance, beauty, dreams, and innocence. The only love that I knew was unconditional, steadfast, and real in my life came from my sister and my little pet Chihuahua, Puff. They could give me warm, fuzzy feelings and bring a smile to my face.

I tried to make sense of the confusing and contradicting thoughts that swirled in my head. My diary was also the one way I had to vent about the secrets I was keeping. These secrets were too dark to be brought into the light. Just in case, I wrote sloppily or used code words when referring to them, so prying eyes wouldn't be able to tell what I was talking about. The last thing I wanted was to be confronted about the dark secrets. That thought terrified me. The fear of not being believed or, even worse, blamed played over and over in my head.

Then one day while I was at school, my mother found my hiding spot and read it. As I walked home, I knew trouble was coming. As often happened, I had an intuition and sense of dread in the pit of my stomach. I had written about my sister and me sneaking around and lying about where we had been. I wrote about us smoking cigarettes, drinking, and being with boys. When she confronted me, I did what all good little Catholic girls did, I "'fessed, up."

I had that virtue beaten into me. I did not want to burn in hell for lying. Thank goodness she hadn't been able to decipher the secrets - or maybe she had and didn't want to go there. Of course, I was grounded for quite awhile. It didn't take much for them to find reason to ground us. If we answered with an attitude, looked at them the wrong way, was ungrateful, disrespectful, or raised our voice, we were grounded for two weeks. That betrayal took away my desire to express myself in a diary ever again.

Then I tried to express my feelings by dabbling with poetry in high school. I wasn't too bad at it. I whimsically wrote as the naïve, sentimental, inexperienced girl that I was. My sense of humor was evident as the rhyming in my poem came easily and was often silly.

When my brothers went into the service, I wrote many letters to them, and they responded. Their letters gave me a peek into their personalities. Their thoughts were like precious jewels to me. I tried to remember their voices as I slowly read each word. We had been separated at such a young age. I tried to get to know them and make up for all the years we had lost.

I wouldn't pick up the pen again to write in earnest until college. I completed college later in life. I wasn't the traditional student, young and fresh out of high school. I had been married and had four children. Although I was still trying to find my way in life, I knew I wanted to use my education to help my people in some way. I wanted to be an advocate and the voice for those who could not speak up for themselves. I felt an urgency to make a difference in the world in some way. I believe it is our destiny to find our niche in life and leave this world in a little better place than it was when we came in.

Many people complimented me on my writing, not so much my college writing, but my letters to the editor. I wrote fervently to the editor of *The L'Anse Sentinel,* the local "mag," that many enjoyed reading to catch up on the latest community gossip. It was during a time when passions were inflamed on the reservation. People said they liked what I had to say and how I said it.

Social injustices had led to a hostile takeover on the reservation. The disruption came about when tribal gaming brought an increase in revenue to the reservation and those in charge sought to keep their power at all costs. When tribal members tried to speak out against what they felt was corruption and abuse of power, they were treated harshly. I was in a position where I had nothing left to lose, and so I became one of the voices that dared to speak up. I wrote what was on the minds of many who feared the consequences if they spoke it publicly. I listened to their stories, examples, and opinions, then wrote from my heart. I tried to write in a way that would encourage the opposition to stop and question what they were doing and to consider the ramifications of their actions.

I've wanted to write a book for a long time, but writing from the heart can be very difficult and painful. Perhaps that's why I've started this book many times but could not finish. As I recalled the traumatic events in my life, the emotional pain that I once buried so deep surfaced once again and became overwhelming. I didn't know how a heart could survive being broken so many times and still keep beating. I finally got my thoughts all out on paper. As I do draft after draft, I find myself having to walk away from the process for awhile. I started having flashbacks that filled me with fear, self-doubt, and self-hatred once again.

Therapists have diagnosed this as Post-Traumatic Stress Disorder. Many associate this disorder to veterans returning from war. That experience has its own horror, but so does living a tortured life of psychological, physical, sexual, spiritual and cultural abuse perpetrated by people who are supposed to love you. The anxiety disorder can manifest in other victims that have experienced or witnessed trauma from accidents, natural disasters, or assaults. The reaction to these memories can feel as real as the first time they happened. Suddenly a familiar sight, sound, smell, comment, touch, or a look can take me to a place that I do not want to go. My insecurities and mistrust of people comes rushing back. It is something I will deal with for the rest of my life.

I had to make peace with all of that and concentrate more on the fact that I'm no longer a victim. I am a survivor and stronger because of my experiences. I've seen and lived through rampant alcoholism, poverty, prejudice, and violence. But I was not alone. I could hardly feel sorry for myself when I knew my brothers, sisters, and cousins, our people, were all pretty much going through the same hardships. I know that there are other people in this country, and all over the world, fighting to hang on to life for just one more day. I may have had it bad, but had it good in the eyes of those living in undeveloped countries where trauma victims must also deal with war, famine, and disease. If we can't find something to be grateful for then we're not looking hard enough.

My Native American heritage is one of the factors why many adults that had control over my life mistreated me. In spite of that fact, I proudly profess that I am a Native American. I've never denied it. It would be hard to deny, anyway. One look at my dark hair, dark eyes, dark skin and high cheekbones gives away my ethnicity. I was proud to be Indian when being Indian wasn't cool, unlike some, who denied their Native ethnicity, until they found out there might be a benefit or discount. Then they were happy to claim their "per cap" payment, their deer license, teeth cleaning, a job, or some other benefit. It is only then that they discover that their grandmother was "an Indian princess." Most Natives laugh at this suggestion because they know we didn't have kings, queens, or other such royalty.

Ojibwa and Oneida blood runs through my veins. And a little Polish blood. I've had to seek out what it means to be an Indian because my culture and identity, among other things, was stolen from me. We were taken from our birthparents that would have raised us to live the traditional lifestyle. The nuns at the boarding school, and later our White adopted parents, forbade us to have anything to do with our Indian culture. They shamed us, ridiculed us, or punished us if we slipped up and did something "Indian." I had no sense of belonging or pride.

I've found out along the way that it really is like living in two worlds. There is a proverb: "One foot cannot stand on two boats." I've also heard the Indian adaptation, "One cannot stand with both feet in two canoes for very long." It is a difficult thing to do, to deny yourself, if you're an Indian, and have to live life as if you are a White person. Sooner or later, you must choose which canoe to stand in, or risk falling into the water, metaphorically speaking.

My adopted parents were very intimidated by my background and my biological family, so, they wouldn't allow me to have anything to do with my relatives. They bad-mouthed my real parents quite often. They did not trust our birth parents. They thought they would come and "steal" my sister and me and take us back to the reservation. Once we were taken from our family, we rarely got to see our relatives and had to wait until we reached legal age to find them again. Our culture, traditions, customs, and language became lost to us. When we went back to the reservation, our friends and relatives would laugh at us for not knowing the old ways.

The government used the institutions of Social Services and the courts to determine how my socialization into mainstream America would proceed. The Catholic Church was equally influential in destroying our identity and instilling new values through the use of brainwashing, threats and intimidation. I had to find my way back and come full circle to be healed. I was born red, but forced to live as if I were white, and experienced plenty of blues in between. I guess, you could say, I am a true patriot.

My birth parents lacked the education, finances, and support to get their kids back. They were caught up in a life of poverty, alcoholism, and ignorance, and eventually just gave up. They had to accept the fact that maybe we were better off, like the social workers, nuns, priests, and judges kept telling them. Maybe all of these White people could give us a better life than they could. They were powerless to fight the system and did not have any control over our future. I soon followed in my parents' footsteps. The term, "learned helplessness," started at an early stage in my life.

I have suffered much heartache, but by the grace of God, somehow got through it. The pain has been replaced with love from my family. God has blessed me with so much, but most cherished, is my loving husband and my four beautiful children. I have three sons and a daughter. My heart swells with pride with what they've accomplished in their lives, in spite of all the dysfunction their father and I have passed onto them. They are much better parents than what they had and have beautiful families of their own. They've spread their wings and didn't let fear stop them from venturing out into the world. Their beautiful souls have touched many lives and have spread much love. They have given me 16 adorable and awesome grandchildren, so far. I told them what was told to me and taught in the Bible, "Be fruitful and multiply." Since then, they have been busy "replenishing the earth."

It has been a long, up-hill journey to the land of self-love. Many factors and people have beaten me down along the way. At times, I have struggled to get back up, for it seemed easier just to stay down. I was determined to prove them wrong. Today, I have many accomplishments of which I'm very proud.

Just as our ancestors persevered, I have persevered, and now my children and their children will persevere, with new challenges to face in a very different world. Our Indian bloodline continues, though it has been thinned out through inter-marriage. I found my answer of what it means to be Indian. It starts with what is in your heart. If it is a kind, generous, and humble heart, then you will live your life as such. One day my children and grandchildren may find themselves asking the same question, "I know Indian blood pumps through my veins, but what does that mean?" I cannot say what answers they will find.

My children did not get to know their grandparents very well on my side of the family, neither did I, for that matter. Their father and I got divorced when they were young. Their father's strict; Polish/Catholic side of the family had more of an influence in their lives. They held the same fears, mistrust, suspicions, and prejudices that my adopted family had toward the Indians, so it seemed.

I write this story so that it might help bridge that gap of misunderstanding. Our people have survived the threat of extinction, wars, famines, mistreatment, racism and prejudices. The government set the tone for people's attitudes toward Natives through the many failed policies. They may have broken our treaties, broken our culture, broken up our families, and yet, they could not break our spirits.

I have heard it said, and now agree, that if other ethnic groups lose their traditions and customs, they can always go back to their homelands to relearn their ways. If ours were to totally disappear, we would have no where to go to relearn the old ways. That is why we fight so desperately for our homeland, our rights, our families, our respect, and our need to keep our culture alive.

What is written in the history books doesn't always reflect the Native American perspective of how the country was founded. It raises a few questions in the minds of our people. How much bravery does it take to kill unarmed, innocent men, women, and children? How much of a conscience is necessary to coldly annihilate a people through germ warfare, torture, starvation, and deprivation? How much integrity should you possess when giving your word and making promises, while knowing full well, that you have no intention of keeping either? How much hypocrisy is required to be able to preach love, honesty, and equality for all, while you are destroying and stealing a people's culture and then lying about it?

The answer is probably not much if you are filled with arrogance, narcissism, and ethnocentrism. Then you can look down your nose, as you hold it high in the air, and ask, "Where have all the full-blooded Indians gone?" What will you tell the Creator as he looks into your eyes and poses that same question? Some of these ideas I've heard in the beautiful lyrics of talented Native American singers like Buddy Red Bow and Floyd Westerman.

These are the same thoughts our famous Chiefs, warriors, grandparents, and Native scholars have been telling us for generations. Sometimes you have to experience something before you can believe it. Now my eyes have been opened.

The story that I am telling, is my best recollection of what, when, and how it happened. I realize that memories fade somewhat as the years past. Some readers may find the language used to be crude, vulgar, offensive, and at times politically incorrect. It is not meant for young readers but for adults that are open-minded and want to be enlightened. The events told might be graphic but it is what actually happened. It is not my intention to hurt anyone's reputation or feelings. It is an account of what happened to me. It is what made me who I am today. Some may not agree with what I write but that is their story to tell, and this is mine.

HISTORY REPEATS ITSELF

My great-grandparents and grandparents lived during a time when the Indian wars were over. Treaties were being made (and broken). The various tribes were being rounded up and forced to live on reservations. A few of the last holdouts had scattered deep into the forests trying to hang on to their culture. Among these, were the Lac Vieux Desert Tribe, a name meaning, "Lake in the Clearing." Still holding on to their traditional way of life, they settled near the Michigan/Wisconsin border, at Lac Vieux Desert, or the Old Village. At that time, Lac Vieux Desert was part of the L'Anse Reservation, later to be called the Keweenaw Bay Indian Community. The Band was one of 12 Bands of Lake Superior Chippewa Indians that signed the Treaty of 1842. They retained their rights to hunt, fish, and gather in the ceded territories of Michigan, Wisconsin, and Minnesota.

Due to the distance from the L'Anse Reservation and given limited resources, Lac Vieux Desert lacked opportunity for growth, jobs, and autonomy. The Lac Vieux Desert Band broke off from the Keweenaw Bay Indian Community and received its own federal recognition in 1988. They acquired more land in the township of Watersmeet, where they built tribal housing, a senior facility, health facility, recreational facility, and other administrative and governmental operations. Growth had finally come to this small community as they began many new ventures. More tribal members choose to stay or return to their reservations given that there were now more opportunities. Success in the gaming industry has had a positive impact by creating jobs and revenue. The metro areas of Green Bay, Milwaukee, and Chicago bring many patrons to the casino/resort.

My grandparents lived off the land and taught their children our traditional ways. Our original traditional ways did not include the use of alcohol. When the Whites introduced alcohol, it became a dominating element in the lives of many Indians. It really was "firewater" to our people. You just did not know what to expect from a "drunken Indian." One theory I heard of why this was so is that the non-Indians had time to acquire a tolerance to alcohol as they sipped a glass or two of wine with their meals. It was their custom to have a celebratory drink now and again. Indians had no acquired tolerance.

Being under the influence, unable to think rationally, and naively thinking that the White man would honor his word, Natives were easily coerced and taken advantage of. We became not only dependent on the government to feed, clothe, and house us, but also became dependent on the substance that numbed out the pain of our losses. Add to that fact that alcohol is a depressant, which lowers the inhibitions, and nothing good can come from that lethal combination. While it aids in temporarily reducing stress and anxiety, individuals under the influence also give no thought as to the consequences of their impulsive behavior. I know because I have personally been there, done that. Consequently, suicide and fatal accidents are statistically higher in the native population. I have witnessed both in my family.

When my parents reached adulthood, the government's policies toward Indians promoted assimilation into the mainstream. Their way of life was slowly being squeezed out of existence. My father had returned home from the war with one more reason to abuse alcohol. Sadly, it wasn't long before domestic violence became a part of their relationship. Our mother finally had enough and eventually left us.

The Relocation Act encouraged Indians to transition to the cities where they could acquire jobs. With the help of government assistance, my mother moved to Milwaukee and got a factory job with Briggs & Stratton. Many Indians accepted city life, but more missed reservation life, where their families were, and returned home. I've learned of these periods in history from many resources while in college. Only now, can I put a name on this face of evil-relocation, assimilation, and degradation. The end result was to "divide and conquer." Our great-grandparents, grandparents, and parents were forced to abide by the government's instituted policies. Now my generation faces the modern results of those same policies.

The government and missionaries still ran boarding schools to house Indian children during the '60s and '70s. I was surprised to learn that Indian boarding schools still exist today in different parts of the country. Times have changed from long ago and these schools are now run quite differently. Some are now tribally-run and some are still funded by the Bureau of Indian Affairs. The federal laws today are now structured to promote our culture. Classes taught such as native language, basket-making, drum circles, regalia-making, etc. help ensure that "the old ways" are not forgotten.

If only we had that opportunity. Just about every one of us from Watersmeet was forced to attend Holy Childhood School in Harbor Springs, MI. It opened in 1829 and finally closed the doors, due to low enrollment, in 1983. But not before destroying hundreds or maybe thousands of lives. Painful stories have been documented concerning the physical and sexual abuse at the hands of the nuns. By stripping us of our identities and breaking up our families, they found it easier to manipulate and assimilate us into the mainstream. Some might call that oppression, and rightfully so, but the government and missionaries believed it was for our own good.

Our parents continued to drink themselves into oblivion over the pain, guilt, and inability to control their own destiny or their children's. If they did not comply, they would have their meager government rations taken away, threatened with jail time, or have the younger children still at home taken from them. When we returned home from there, we began to drink excessively, also. Alcoholism, depression, and suicide were commonplace on most reservations. Today the rates are still high on a per capita basis. Being taken from their families, mistreated, abused, and the loss of our culture, took its toll on a once proud people.

However, the Civil Rights Era, brought about advances that were more humane in the way our government dealt with the tribes. The passing of the

Indian Child Welfare Act in the late 1970's, allowed native children to remain together with family, relatives, and in the Native community. The premise was to promote the values of Indian culture and elevate their sense of identity. At last, what was in the best interest of the child was taken into account.

Our people have become better educated. The high school drop-out rate for our youth has declined with more graduating from high school and going on to college. Even more are obtaining graduate degrees. Many have built professional careers and have obtained positions where they can better represent tribal interests. We have made great strides in court actions to redress some of the wrongs. Through litigation we have won protections for our treaty rights, mineral rights, and repatriation of Indian remains and artifacts. Reader's Digest was a helpful resource as they discussed these issues of contemporary Indians in their book, "America's Fascinating Indian Heritage."

Beginning in the late 1960's and early 1970's, the American Indian Movement became influential in bringing about a resurgence of our culture in religion, ceremonies, language, and the arts. Although controversial, AIM brought Native issues to the forefront through their activism. Some may consider AIM to be too radical in their approach, still others consider them modern-day warriors fighting for their brothers and sisters, regardless of what tribe you are from. They do not believe a pacifist attitude gets you heard or respected. That is how I have interpreted this social movement. A good read that describes the American Indian Movement and the founders is in the book, "Like a Hurricane," by author Paul Chaat Smith. To many of our people today they are considered heroes and are still called upon for advice and assistance.

As a teenager in the 1970s, even though they were in the news, I was not aware of what the Movement was all about. I had the chance to meet some of the AIM leaders when they were asked to come to Baraga twenty some years later. I remember seeing a t-shirt someone was wearing at that time that paid homage to our famous chiefs. The front of the t-shirt read, "Our heroes are your enemies," and had pictures of Sitting Bull, Geronimo, Dennis Banks and Clyde Bellecourt from AIM. The back of the t-shirt read, "Your heroes are our enemies," and had pictures of U.S. Presidents and General Custer. Is that radical? Yes, but point being, that is the type of charismatic leaders it takes to fight for your people and for what you believe in.

Our youth, and the next generations to come, need to know the true story of what our people have gone through to get to where we are today. They must not forget all that we had, what we almost lost of our culture, what we have gotten back, and how to hold on to it. Our future depends upon this. It is just as important today as it was yesterday. The Native values such as caring for each other should be the priority. By helping others, we help ourselves to build character.

Our elected tribal leaders need to remember this fundamental value. While governing and serving their people, they must try to reach out to all members, not just their family and friends.

We are also taught to respect and learn from our elders, for they are our most valuable resource.

Together, we can all do our part in protecting Mother Earth. Even the simple act of keeping her clean by not throwing garbage, wrappers, etc. out of car windows goes a long way. I've traveled through some states that look awful, with garbage lining the side of the road and ditches.

We are fortunate to live in "Pure Michigan," where we can still breathe fresh air, drink clean water and behold beautiful sights.

MY EARLIEST MEMORIES

I was born on October 7, 1958 in Phelps, WI. My family lived in Watersmeet, MI, a very rural area, with a modest population of approximately five hundred, located in the western Upper Peninsula, about 8 miles from the Wisconsin border. Most of the small band of Indians lived out at the Old Village near Lac Vieux Desert, an inland lake set deep into the woods. We lived just outside of town though, about a half-mile or so and just off the highway coming into town from the south.

Some say that we do not have memories or are incapable of remembering before 5 years of age. Well, I have lots of memories before turning 5. Some are only flashes of what happened but some are very clear. I can also remember the emotional pain that went along with those memories.

Our mother, father, aunt and her seven kids or so and my siblings all lived together under one roof. It resembled more a tar-papered shack. Of course, there was no electricity or running water. Our grandmother and grandfather lived right next to us in a tiny trailer. I had two older brothers, Luther, two years older, and Melvin who was born the year before me. Two sisters were born after me, 3 years younger, and the other was five years younger. We lived a simple life, taking only what we needed from the land to survive.

My grandfather worked in the woods cutting pulp. Grandfather looked as though he was more White than Indian, but he was half Chippewa also. His name was Frank Brunk, Sr. He was half-Polish but lived his life more like the natives. I recall him as being partially balding and he had only one eye that was blue. Grandfather taught my father how to hunt, trap, fish, cut wood, and everything a man needed to know to support his family. My grandfather and grandmother had seven children. Five were boys, one who was killed in a car accident, and two were girls.

My grandmother was a small, round woman who looked native and was tough as nails. She was full-blooded Ojibwa, or Chippewa. She wore her long dark hair pulled back in a bun. She loved to chew tobacco. I remember she had one tooth left on the bottom and usually a wad was stuck in her lip. The smell and sight of brown tobacco juice trickling out of the corner of her mouth was quite yucky. She would get a kick out of watching us gag as she would spit right next to your bare foot.

She always wore long dresses below her knee with hosery rolled up above her knee. She wore an apron over that. Her apron had a pocket where she carried a handkerchief folded up. In that handkerchief she seemed to pull out everything but the kitchen sink. Whether it was money, medicine, pins, whatever you needed, she seemed to have it in that handkerchief. She mostly spoke Ojibwa. Like many of the elders, she had a wealth of knowledge about plants, roots, herbs, and medicines. Grandmother knew which of these were edible and which could be used to cure ailments. Some say she was a Medicine woman. Grandma delivered most of her grandchildren. Our family still lived the traditional life of performing ceremonies, tanning hides, trapping, hunting, gathering, drumming, singing Indian songs around the campfire, and keeping to our own.

My mother told me that once my grandmother cast some sort of spell on a woman. She said that my aunt and another woman were in love with the same man. My grandma did a "shakey-tent" ceremony and made the other woman go crazy. The other woman's family performed a ceremony to address the "bad medicine." It was said that my grandmother's face appeared in the smoke. They knew then that she had made their daughter go insane.

As kids, we were always running through the woods barefooted and playing in the nearby creeks and rivers, unsupervised. On nice nights, we all sat around a fire outside. Our parents were very lenient. There was such a sense of freedom to run wild with few rules. We were left to explore and experience our world on our own. We became familiar with the four-legged, two-legged, and winged creatures that lived amongst us.

There was a creek not far into the woods behind our house. My mother use to take us down there to play while she washed our clothes. As a young child I was very small and petite. The creek probably only came up to the knees of an adult but to me it seemed like the creek was a river. I would mud-crawl, dragging myself up the creek yelling, "Look at me, I'm swimming!"

Sometimes we would look for wild strawberries to pick for breakfast. We would also find blueberries, raspberries, chokecherries, wintergreens, and apples to pick and munch on for energy during the day. All of the running and playing was exhausting. Once we found an old road sign lying on the ground, so we started dancing naked and singing "whoo, whoo, whoo," while running around the sign. That's what we saw the adults doing around the fire to the beat of the drum. It was on hot, summer nights that they took their shirts off, sweating profusely, as they danced and sang to the beat of the drum. To us, it seemed as though they were naked, so we did the same, mimicking them.

Generally, we just tried to stay out of the way of the adults. They would all get together and party hearty, drink, and fight. Alcoholism was bad on the reservation. We really didn't know what to expect once they started getting loud. It was not uncommon for them to start out drinking amiably only to wind up having knock-down-drag-out fights by the end of the night. The next day they would laugh about the night before.

My mom told me that we lived in a smaller shack before the bigger, tar-paper shack was built. One night when they were drinking, my father wanted to go home, but my mother didn't, so he told her if she didn't come home right then that she would not have a home to come home to. She didn't come home, and sure enough, he had burnt the house down.

No one cared if we got hold of a beer and staggered around after a few sips. It started out with us going around picking up the empties and finishing the bottom of the beers. They laughed hysterically at our antics. I was told they would put wine in our bottles so we would go to sleep, and they could party. Our grandmother knew how to make homemade choke cherry and dandelion wine. No wonder many of us grew up to become alcoholics.

My mother told me a story about when I was a baby. She said that they were all drinking, and I wouldn't go to sleep. I kept crying and crying. I was lying in a hammock made out of a blanket. She got tired of pushing me, so she gave me a big swing, thinking it would keep me going for a little longer. Instead, I was flipped out and then hit the floor. She laughed as she told the story, but all I could think was, wow, guess the abuse started early. Maybe she was laughing at herself for being so thoughtless. Or, maybe she was trying to "toughen" me up in preparation for what I would have to face later.

We were too poor to have any toys like bikes, balls, or dolls. We used our imagination and made our own toys. The boys made bow and arrows, spears, snares, hatchets, and tied ropes in the trees for swings. We would hide in the trees and throw rocks and apples at cars and trucks going by on the highway. Once, our cousins must have broken somebody's truck window because the driver stopped to tell my uncle. We all took off out into the woods to hide behind trees, under logs, or in the bushes. Our uncle hollered to his kids and us that we had better come out. "You may as well break a switch off on your way in because you're going to get a whooping," he yelled to us. Our relatives were allowed to give us an ass-beating too, if we needed one.

We used little blocks of wood and pretended they were toy cars, and built our own little roads in the sand. There were no birthday parties for anyone. We didn't celebrate Christmas or any of the other holidays. Our families were very traditional. Those holidays were the white man's beliefs, not ours. Besides, how can you miss what you've never had?

The boys were incessant in their quest for snakes, spiders, and bugs to scare the girls by throwing them on us or chasing us with them. I still can't stand creepy, crawly things. They were taught how to snare rabbits, trap beaver, muskrat, weasels, shoot deer and spear fish.

I wouldn't get to participate in a lot of the games they played because

I was too little. One of my older cousins would say, "Do you want to play, Linda? Yes means no, and no means yes." If I said yes, I didn't get to play. So I would say no and she would say, "O.K. then, you said no, so you don't want to play." Another cousin, who was her older brother, in his teens, also teased me. He would tell me, "Linda, come here, I have something for you." I would run over thinking it was candy or money. He seemed so tall that all he had to do was bend his knees to sit on my head, and then he farted. It would be loud and sounded like someone was ripping a sheet in half. Everyone in the room busted out laughing. It's not like we knew what a sheet was back then because we didn't have any. We stayed warm with the old green, itchy, wool blankets.

They would both make me cry, so I would go play with my sister, who was ever smaller than I was. We would fight, too. One time my mother said she came crying to her saying, "Mommy, Linda scratched me." My mom told her, "Well, scratch her back." She said I turned my back to her and said, "Ya, scratch my back."

My uncle and aunt with their 8 kids lived a hop, skip, and a jump from us. Just down from them lived another of our aunts, her husband and their 8 or 9 kids. Another of our aunts lived with us. She must have had about 6 kids, mostly older boys who were teenagers, and two girls. All of the cousins were close in age. So, we didn't need friends, we had plenty of relatives to play with. Our house had three bedrooms. My aunt and our parents had their own small bedrooms. Her kids had a bedroom in the back of the house. The small kitchen/living room was where we slept on the couch, Luther, Melvin, my younger sister, and me.

It's funny how you think you hear something a certain way and sometimes you do not find out until years down the road how wrong you were. For instance, I must have been about 3 or 4 and I thought everyone was calling our aunts Boob and Steve, I didn't find out until in my twenties that their nicknames were Aunt Bood and Aunt Steeb. All of the adults spoke Indian (Ojibway), as well as English.

Our grandmother's name was Martha. Her nickname was Gabo. I think the nicknames were actually a shortened version of their Indian names. Most Indian names were very long with many syllables. Grandmother wasn't so fond of her daughter-in-laws. One of my aunts was a big woman, Indian, but from another tribe. Grandma would walk behind her and stomp her feet, and swing her arms like a monkey, mocking her. My mother was from the Oneida Tribe, fairer-skinned, and grandma called her, "that white Oneida bitch".

I always felt like grandma didn't like kids and didn't want us around her. I saw her sitting on the front step one day and wanted to sit by her. I started to walk toward her when she yelled at me, "majohn," and gave a wave of her hand. I thought she was saying "by john," you know, like "by George, by John." Years later someone who spoke Ojibwa laughed and said she was saying "majon," which means "get out of here, or get away."

Grandma was not afraid to speak her mind and had no tolerance for insincerity from people. One of my older cousins, in his thirties, once tried to "suck up" to her saying, "Gee, Grandma Martha, that's a pretty dress...where'd you get it from?" "I pulled it out of my cunt, anything else you want to know?" No, she wasn't one much for compliments, and she didn't appreciate being spoken to as if she were a child. She didn't learn any couth, as she got older, either. If someone made her mad by telling her she had enough beer, she would say, "Ah, fuck my shit!" Most people would be left standing with their mouth's hanging open, but our relatives thought it was so funny.

My grandfather was a hard worker and taught his sons everything he knew. They were self-sufficient. They could raise chickens, fish, trap, hunt, and cut wood. Michigan winters were, and still are, hard, but we were accustomed to a life of hardship and inconvenience. I don't remember anyone complaining about what we didn't have, though. There was only acceptance and gratitude for being alive and all that the Creator did give to us. They thanked Him for the animals that gave their lives so that we might live. They thanked Him for the waters that gave us the fish to eat, clean our clothes with, drink, and clean ourselves. They thanked Him for our health and strength that we needed to do what needed to get done. They thanked Him for our family and for another day in this beautiful place where He put us. I wasn't aware at the time, but they were teaching me a very important lesson that I would realize the meaning of, one day. That is, everything and everybody has a purpose in this circle of life.

We heated with wood in a pot-belly stove that sat towards the center of the house. We also cooked on it during the winter and warmed up our water. We carried water from another source nearer to the house, a shallow, hand-dug well. We burned kerosene lanterns and the bathroom was an outhouse. Everyone pitched in to get the chores done.

We were told grandpa was from the Rooster Clan and grandma was from the Bear Clan. I didn't know there was a rooster clan. I thought it had more to do with how they teased each other so mercilessly. Grandpa, being half-white, was told he was from the cock clan.

Grandpa took his pelts and hides to the trading post in L'Anse, across the bay from Baraga. He and my dad actually walked the 60 miles, or so, to the post on the old Lac Vieux Desert Trail. They would stop and camp along the way. The trail has long been overgrown, but I heard it was being resurrected through a grant. I was told that my grandfather would tell my dad stories on the long trek about Wendigo, a spirit that lived in the woods. The evil spirit would catch children, torment them if they had been bad, before killing them and then eating them. He had my dad so scared that he was practically walking on his heels all the way.

One of the few memories I have of grandpa was when we thought he was shooting at us in the woods. We were all playing on the trails between our houses and got the bright idea to throw rocks at our grandparents' trailer. We wanted to see who could hit it and listened for the noise as they hit the tin on the trailer or landed on the roof. It must have really pissed grandpa off because the next thing you know, he came out with his shotgun and fired up into the air. We thought he was shooting at us and we all scattered and took off running in different directions.

My mother told me he was a very jealous man. He had tried to shoot himself over my grandmother. He aimed for his head but instead took out his eye. I guess he had tried to hang himself one time too, but the rope broke. Our grandfather ultimately died of a heart attack in the summer of 1965, the same summer my sister and I were taken to Baraga. I remember all of the relatives were over by our house on the day of his passing.

We all lived in poverty. No one had more than the others did. It was an uncomplicated and happy life in the world we lived. I remember that the inside of our house smelled similar to being outdoors. The thick smell of kerosene lanterns burning, the smoke from the potbelly stove, and the stench of the hides drying inside were constant. I do remember being scared when I had to go to the bathroom because it was so dark outside. Once I saw something big and black. I must have startled a bear that took off running. I went running in the opposite direction straight back into the house.

It felt like we all lived as one big family. We were so carefree with few worries. We ran through the woods, climbed trees, splashed in the water, chased little animals, and just amused ourselves with our cousins. The bottoms of our feet were like leather from going bare-footed. It didn't even phase us when we ran on gravel. I remember we would try to make others laugh by running through the snow with no shoes on.

Besides the heavy drinking, domestic violence was another factor in our lives. We saw our mother take some awful beatings at the hands of our father. I suppose he was a jealous man also, like my grandfather. My father didn't hesitate to take his belt off and tan our hides either, no pun intended, when he thought we deserved it. Whether it was his belt or a willow switch, they both left welts that hurt like hell.

Our mother and father weren't married legally, but rather lived the traditional Indian way. When someone stayed with another for years and had children with that person, they were considered to be married, similar to "common law." This was my father's second marriage. He was about 10 years older than my mother. Mom must have been about 17 or 18 when she met him. He had moved back to Watersmeet, from Kansas, after getting out of the service. Our mother was an attractive woman. My father dropped his girlfriend like a hot potato when he set eyes on her. His first marriage was to a Mexican woman, and they had two girls together. They had lived in Kansas so we never really knew our half-sisters.

My father was a man who was small in stature, could speak 5 languages, and had served seven years in the army. He served in WWII and the Korean Conflict. He was 17 years old when he volunteered; the same age our brothers were when they joined the service. He was multi-lingual and had a high IQ but was a humble and quiet man. He always had a joke or funny story to tell, too. You had to listen closely though because he mumbled when he spoke.

While serving overseas, he had learned to speak Italian and French, which he said were similar languages. Father learned Spanish while he was married to his first wife. Of course, Ojibwa was his first language. He learned English from the orphanage run by missionaries in Baraga, when he was a child. He wasn't an orphan but apparently the government's policies of assimilation affected even him. He said grandpa quit sending him there because his right arm was getting larger than his left arm. When I asked him how that could happen, he said it was from making the sign of the cross so often. He had the greatest sense of humor. Everyone in my family was hilarious. Someone was always ripping on someone or themselves. We shared many laughs. There was always a lot of teasing going on. Teasing is a way of showing how well you are liked in our culture.

I remember my dad giving me a good ass-whooping when he caught me near the road one day. Our driveway was just off the highway. I must have been about 4 years old. I went to the end of the driveway to look towards town to see if I could see my father walking home. I could see a figure coming my way and by the way he moved, I knew that it was our dad. I started to walk towards him to meet him. I knew not to walk on the road. I was walking on the side of the road. As he walked closer I could see him waving one arm like crazy. He was motioning for me to get off the road. I wasn't sure what he wanted because I was already off the road. I moved to the grass anyway, and he was still swinging his arm. I then moved down towards the ditch. He was just about up to me when he also went to the ditch and snapped off a switch from a tree. That's when I knew I was going to get it. He got up to me and started whipping my backside with it. "Didn't I tell you never to go by the road?" Well, I didn't make that mistake again.

I remember all of us would get together and take a ride on the backroads to go looking for "greens" also known as princess pine. I don't know where the car came from because I don't think we had one. We picked the greens by hand, they came up easily, and then we stuffed them into gunnysacks. Our parents would sell them down at the local gas station and were paid by the pound. A company from Wisconsin would come up to buy the greens. They would be used to make Christmas wreaths. Our parents would use the money to buy beer and liquor. That is one of the more fond memories I have of the happier times when I was young. Our families were all together doing something that everyone could participate in. It was fun for our moms, dads, sisters, brothers and our cousins.

I can remember us going to the dump as another family outing. Before the landfills, communities had open dumpsites. Sometimes people would go there to watch the bears rummaging through the garbage. Sometimes our trips there were to see what we could scrummage and bring home. As a matter of fact, my mother told me that my first dress came from the dump. She found a big doll that wore a pretty dress. She took it off the doll, brought it home, washed it up, and put it on me. It fit me like a glove. I about cried when she told me that story. I thought, how pathetic that the only nice thing she could get me, came from the dump. She mostly dressed me in hand-me-downs from my brothers.

That is also where we found a couch and hauled it home. It was our bed, not the pull-out kind either, for my two brothers, my sister, and I to sleep on. When they told us, "goodnight, don't let the bedbugs bite," they meant it literally. I still have scars on my arms from scratching the scabs off.

One day, with nothing else to do, we pulled the couch out from the wall, took all of our clothes off, and started whoo, whoo, whooing, slapping our hand on our mouths, while running around the couch, just as we had with the road sign. Our grandma came in and saw us. She was really mad and yelled at us to get our clothes back on. We thought that was what wild, little Indians did.

One night, that I'll never forget, is when my father beat my mother up so badly, she lay bleeding on the floor. He had knocked her out but continued punching and kicking her and whipping her with his belt. There was nothing she could do to protect herself. We were all crying and screaming for him to stop. He yelled at us shouting, "Shut up or I'll use this on you!" It wasn't long after that she took our youngest sister, who she was nursing at the time, and left us. She probably feared for her life, and rightfully so. My father might very well have gotten carried away and killed her. Her brothers came to get her and took her back to Wisconsin where their tribe, the Oneida, were from. That was the last we saw of her except for a couple of occasions. Eventually, she moved to Milwaukee.

After my sister and I became adults, we looked her up and started to rebuild our relationship with her. She had brothers and sisters, but I did not get to know my aunts, uncles, and cousins or grandparents from her side of the family. Years later, as an adult I would get to meet some of them. She was still our mother, and I could not hold any hatred toward her. I figured she did what she had to do. I'm sure that she probably went through her own hell with her decision.

Mom had gotten a good union job at Briggs and Stratton after she left my dad, and she worked there until she retired. Soon after retiring, her diabetes got worse. A genetic disposition and years of drinking eventually brought about a stroke. She had to go on dialysis, became bedridden, and ended up in a nursing home where she passed away in 2009. Though we had a strained relationship, a lot of healing had taken place. She met her grandchildren and came to visit a few times. My sisters and I visited her as often as we could.

Diabetes was rampant on both sides of the family. One of our aunts, our dad's sister, had her leg partially amputated due to her diabetes. My uncle, on my mother's side died an early death at 38, from having untreated diabetes.

The day our mother left my father and us, and took our youngest sister, is still etched in my brain. The rest of us were all crying uncontrollably, holding on to her, begging her to stay or take us with her. "Please mommy, don't go," we all cried. She was crying, too, as she told us that she loved us but had to go. I don't know how I got through that, because it made my heart ache. It actually felt like I had been stabbed in the chest. I guess we got through it by knowing that we still had each other. Dad, my sister, and my brothers still made up part of a family. Things would never be the same in our little lives. That would be the first of many losses to bear.

After she left, I can remember something odd happening as I slept in the same bed with my father. Even at that young age, I knew he was doing something peculiar. I was just about asleep when I awoke to find him under the covers. I could see a dim light under the blankets as he lit a match. I laid there motionless, confused as to what he was doing. I had the feeling he was looking at my privates down there. I didn't know what to make of it. I just knew it didn't feel right as I slowly drifted off to sleep.

I don't have many more memories after that, not happy ones, anyway, of Watersmeet. Not too much time had passed when a priest came, driving a van, to pick us all up. All of the cousins were going to be rounded up and taken downstate to a boarding school. When we saw the van approaching we all scattered into the woods to hide. We stayed until enough time had passed that we thought he would be gone. We came back, expecting to see him gone. To our dismay, there he sat, waiting patiently, knowing we would have to come out sooner or later. Our families were being torn apart. Those carefree days had come to an end. Our hearts were being broken, again, and there was nothing any of us could do about it.

HARBOR SPRINGS BOARDING SCHOOL

The Indian boarding school was located in Harbor Springs, MI. It was called Holy Childhood of Jesus, a Catholic school, that was run by nuns. We were sent there for the school year and were able to go home for the summer. It was about a five or six hour drive from Watersmeet. The most terrifying part of the ride for me was when we had to cross over the Mackinaw Bridge. I hadn't ever been on a bridge that large or had ever seen so much water. I was petrified and remember lying on the floor of the van, crying, too scared to look out the window. All I could think was that if the van fell off the bridge, it was a long way down to the water.

After a number of years, we became known as, "Watersmeet trash" at the boarding school. I guess it was because most of our boys would start fighting as soon as their feet hit the ground with anyone who said the wrong thing to them. Actually, the girls too, would scrap. We all had a chip on our shoulder from being taken from our parents and the insolence was plain to see on our faces. Watersmeet Indians were known not to like anyone. They didn't even like other Indians. I think the animosity came from the fact that we felt as though we may have had to put up with the adults treating us badly, but we weren't about to take it from the other kids.

The school authorities had to track down a few of us who had tried to run away and go back home. The run-aways would only make it hitchhiking as far as the Mackinac Bridge and then they couldn't get a ride to the other side. They would be brought back to do their time at Harbor. Their punishment would be harsh beatings or they were made to kneel for hours, praying for forgiveness. There were some that were made to repeat the whole school year. It was just like being sentenced to prison. Our freedom had been taken.

The nuns were from the order of Sisters of Notre Dame. Their black habits fell to the floor, with the inside of their white veils showing only their faces. They sure were sweet and nice when we arrived. I thought that maybe it wouldn't be such a bad place. We would have to make the best of it and think of it as a new adventure.

The building was made of brick and stood three stories high. They gave us the grand tour of our new home. On the third floor were the dormitories where we now would live. One half was for the girls and the other half was for the boys. On the second floor were classrooms where we would learn to read, write, learn to speak English only, and study the bible like good little Indians. Our music classes taught us to sing songs for church. The cafeteria was located on the bottom floor. A lounge or television room was also on the lower floor. The church was located next door, and we had to attend mass daily, first thing in the morning.

We all sat alphabetically at the tables for meals. At least we got to sit with family, be near each other, and remember what it was like when we spent our days running through the woods. We would smile at each other across the table, but quickly dropped our smile as the nuns patrolled the room. We were careful not to talk about home if one of the nuns were within earshot.

The school was run more like a military boot camp. The nuns could have put any drill instructor to shame. Their long black habits concealed what looked like combat boots underneath. We had glimpses of them when they hiked up their habits to put the boots to us. One of my cousins says she remembers one of the nuns picking her up and throwing her across the room. She said she went skidding across the floor. I asked her, "Why do you think they did that?" She said that she didn't remember, probably because she wasn't moving fast enough. I remember when a kid was in trouble, they would be shouting that we were, "good for nothing, stinking little, dirty Indians."

Gone were the days of running wild and free with no rules. There would be so many new rules to learn that it was impossible to remember them all. But, they would beat us every time we forgot one so, we learned quickly. The paralyzing fear would overcome me as I worried that I would make the wrong move. I started to crawl into a shell thinking that if I kept my mouth shut and eyes down, they wouldn't see me or find a reason to raise a hand to me.

Every frickin' day, we would have cornmeal mush for breakfast. They fed us lots of things I couldn't choke down, but we had to eat everything on our plate or sit there until we did. I hated beets, and I remember sitting and crying in my plate until it got dark outside. They finally sent me to bed. One of my cousins felt sorry for me at times and would eat some of the things for me, so I wouldn't be punished.

The boys were made to wear little wool blazers to church all year long. Sometimes it would get so hot they would be kneeling with hands praying, and then just keel over.

I remember all of the beds in the dorm were lined up straight in rows. We all had a little nightstand and chair next to our bed. Our clothes would be laid out on the chair with what we were expected to wear the next day. We had the same routine every day: wake up, dress, wash, brush our teeth, make your bed, and then line up to go downstairs to church. You were expected to march single file and not dare to step out of line.

The nuns would come by to inspect our beds to make sure they were made properly. That is where I learned how to make hospital corners, at 5 years of age, and in first grade. There wasn't a wrinkle in my bed. I saw it happen too many times. If a quarter didn't bounce off your bed, it would get ripped apart for you to make again. God forbid, one girl use to wet the bed, they made her scrub the entire bathroom floor with her toothbrush on her hands and knees.

I use to cry myself to sleep sometimes, but was careful not to utter a sound for fear of getting beaten for that. I could hear the sniffles from other girls crying in the dark, too. My heart longed to be home with my family. My brothers must have been attending public school in Watersmeet at that time. They attended Harbor Springs also. Our dad probably gave them a break for a year or so. My younger sister was too little to be in school yet, but would be sent as soon as she was old enough.

The memories of that place still haunt me. It infuriated me how the nuns could make adults believe that they were excellent caretakers. Only we knew their true nature. The nuns would make us write home and tell us what to write. "Dear daddy, we like it here, the nuns are nice to us, etc." Some parents would send their kids presents or other things but the nuns wouldn't let them have them. When parents came to visit at Christmas, the nuns would bring out their missing things and give them to the kids before their parents got there, as if the kids had them all along. They would be taken away again after the parents left. I, of course never got anything, my dad couldn't afford to send anything, but I still felt sorry for the other kids who wanted something from home.

The nun who was our dorm mother was called Sister N. She had a laugh that sounded exactly like I remembered my mother's laugh, kind of squeaky. I felt as though she was my surrogate mom. I told her that one time when she came to tell me goodnight. "You sound just like my mom," I said. She kind of had a little soft spot for me after that.

In May, we celebrated the crowning of Mary, Queen of Heaven. There was a little celebration outside where a statue of Mary, Mother of God, would be crowned. One girl would be picked to carry the crown on a satin pillow and walk it up to the statue. Well, guess who was chosen? I was so proud. A pretty little blue dress was picked out for me to wear. The day came and everyone was rushing around getting ready. It was somewhat chaotic. My dress was not laid out on my chair; it was hanging on a rack in the back, where no one told me I could find it. I was starting to panic and cry because some of the girls were ready and were beginning to line up already. I knew what I was in for if I held up the group.

Sister N. came and asked me why I wasn't ready. I was sobbing and told her I couldn't find my dress. She screamed at me to quit crying and get ready. With that, she swung and hit me so hard she knocked me to the floor. I screamed and cried all the harder. That's when she started kicking me in the back with those big, black combat boots and hollered, "I said shut up, get up, and get ready!" I picked myself up and got dressed.

By then everyone was lined up and all eyes were on me. They looked at me with pity and probably saw the humiliation on my face. I think they were wishing they could have been the one picked to carry the crown but were glad they weren't chosen, when they saw what happened to me. I somehow got ready and limped up, carrying the crown to the front like I was supposed to as tears streamed down my cheeks. Sister N. sure knew how to take the excitement out of something. It was meant to be an honorable event but turned into one that made a spectacle out of me. I didn't like her much after that. I didn't care anymore if her squeaky laugh did sound like my mother's. I wished I could do to her what she had done to me.

There was a fence around the yard of the school property. It felt like we were caged animals. They treated us as if we were. There was a playground there and all of the children could escape from the nightmare for a little while during recess time. There was one girl that stood out from all of the others. Her name was Susan S. I remember her because she was lighter skinned and had bright, blue eyes. They were the same color as my little sister's and my brother Melvin's. I liked anything that reminded me of home. That familiarity must be the reason Susan's name stood out for me. After all of these years, her name still sticks in my head. It surprised me when, only a few years ago, I ended up working with her brother on Mackinaw Island. We were talking about Harbor Springs. I brought up Susan's name, and he said, "That's my sister!" Isn't it a small world?

The school taught 1st grade through the eighth grade. The dormitories at Harbor Springs had a smaller room for the younger girls and a larger room that was for the older girls. The nun's bedroom was somewhere in the middle. Often, I could see the light on from under their bedroom door. The boy's dorm was set up the same way on the other half of the building. A set of double-doors separated the sections, and we were never allowed through them.

Years later I learned from some of my male cousins that the nuns would bring the older boys into their room at night and have sex with them. I have one cousin who is a bad alcoholic and can't seem to get a woman. In a self-pitying moment he whined, "Boy, I'd kill for a piece of ass right now. Where are those nuns when you need one?" One of our strongest survival skills is our sense of humor. Native people are very good at finding the humor in unbearable situations. But, I thought to myself how we'd all like to have a piece of them today.

Indian children from all over the state attended the school at Harbor Springs. Some non-Indian children attended there also, but most were Native. Parents had absolutely no say over their own children's well being and were powerless to do anything about the abuse. The nuns wanted to change everything about us, how we walked, talked, and dressed. We were treated like we were worthless, useless, nothing better than dogshit stuck to the bottom of someone's shoe. The boys had their long, beautiful hair chopped off, as did the girls. We weren't allowed to speak a word of Indian. If it happened to slip out, they would not hesitate to slap you across the face, leaving a red handprint on your cheek.

Every day we were forced to go to church and listen to the good word of God. Where was He while all of this was going on? I just didn't feel the love. Their behavior was more parallel to what we were taught about the devil and all of his evil deeds. The diocese which had jurisdiction over the Catholic school, sure turned a blind eye to what was occurring. For all of their intellect and self-righteousness, they could not see how many lives the nuns were ruining. We somehow survived that entire episode and came home at the end of the school year. By then the damage was done and our parents became alienated from their children. We were strangers to each other. That was my one and only year, thank God, I had to attend. I felt so sorry for all of the kids who had to keep going back year after year.

To this day, there has not been reparation made to any of these victims that I am aware of. We have looked into a class-action lawsuit against the diocese and any surviving staff but were told the statute of limitations has run out. I believe that the atrocities committed here and at other boarding schools around the country, and in Canada, have been the primary influencing factor in the high rate of alcoholism and suicides on our reservations. People who abuse alcohol do so to forget and dull the pain of what has happened.

Thankfully, the school was finally closed down in 1983. It had been turned into a pre-school and eventually the building was demolished.

I've researched other similar stories and interviews on the Internet of Native children abused at this school. An excellent series by the newsweekly, Northern Express, in 2008, appropriately titled "Unholy Childhood," told of sexual abuse of boys perpetrated by the nuns. While interviewing some 80 Natives, they all had the same resounding theme of "kissing lessons, hickeys, and fondling," they experienced. A couple of the nuns told the boys they thought they might be pregnant. The only response from the spokesperson representing the Sisters of Notre Dame was one of denial and blame. She said the comments came from "troubled," accusers.

The psychological damage from years of mistreatment and the stripping of Native people's identity sometimes becomes irreversible. Fortunately, a few decades ago, the boarding schools were closed and new laws were introduced help to protect our culture. The 1978 federal Indian Child Welfare Act has helped to keep Native families together and allow the healing to begin.

Not too long ago I heard a news story about a white couple adopting an Indian baby down south somewhere. They were in jeopardy of losing the baby because the birth father, a Native American, wanted his daughter back. As you can imagine, the new parents had become attached to the baby. There was a big custody battle because of the Indian Child Welfare Act. Just like our treaties, non-Indians feel this law has become outdated. I felt the media hadn't been objective in giving the full story. Yes, I could feel for the adoptive parents, but given the history many others and myself have gone through, and why the law was implemented in the first place, my sentiments were with the biological father. The white man wants to make the rules, and then doesn't want to live by them when they no longer suit him. The intent of the law was to help keep families together and stop the assault on our culture.

Those of us who have had our culture and innocence stolen from us had to return to the reservation, dishonored, for denying, and not knowing the old ways anymore. Our own friends and relatives may judge us based on our knowledge of being Indian. If you do not know the significance of tobacco, the rituals of ceremony, how to speak your native tongue, the custom of how to make regalia, or how to dance at pow-wows, then, you are not considered to be a traditional Indian. Some may even call you an "apple," red on the outside and white on the inside. Granted, in this day and age, we cannot live as we did 100 years ago, we are a different civilization. However, we should not be shamed while exercising and taking pride in our traditions. We are not mascots or targets to be ridiculed, patronized, or dismissed.

There are many reasons why American Indians, or some of us, have an identity crisis going on internally while we try to find a balance to live in both worlds. I find it frustrating as I try to describe the many factors and aspects that compound this dilemma. It's complicated and confusing when examining man's inhumanity to man. In the name of "progress," our government exterminated tribes and committed genocide. Third World countries still try to control their people in barbaric ways. It takes a war by a superpower to try and stop it. Meanwhile, innocent civilian lives are lost. Where does it end? Will it take an asteroid slamming into our planet or an alien invasion for us to all get along and work together? Will we ever get to a place where we respect our differences, focus on our similarities, and realize how much we can learn from each other? Or, is it inevitable that our planet will come to an end the same way it began, with one big explosion?

As for our country, immigrants have always held to the philosophy that Americans are likened to a great "melting pot". I came across another interesting, and maybe more appropriate analogy many years ago, that our multiculturalism is comparable to a "salad bowl," model. The more distinctiveness each culture provides, and variety, only adds for a more tasty and nutritious result.

ADOPTION AND A BETTER LIFE

I returned home from Harbor Springs beaten down, lonely, and numbed out from missing our mother only to find that our lives were about to change again. We got a visit from a lady named Rose Mansfeldt. She lived on the outskirts of Baraga, MI. This was about an hour north of Watersmeet, around 65 miles, or about a 12-pack. My dad always judged the distance by how much beer they would drink before they got there.

Rose was a middle-aged, white woman who, with the assistance of Social Services, took in Native foster kids. Rose and her husband owned a farm with horses, cows, and chickens. She came bearing gifts for my father, a twelve-pack of beer. As the adults conversed, we wondered what was going on, and why she was there. She said Social Services had received complaints that our dad had these four kids that he couldn't take care of properly and that maybe she could help. Our appearance was probably evident of that, given our unkept, dirty, scrawny, raggedy appearance.

Anyway, she explained that she and her husband provided a temporary home for foster kids while their parents got on their feet. They had lots of land just outside of town near Baraga for kids to run around and play. They were discussing a plan for my sister and me to go live with them. The more my dad drank, the more he considered it, and the next thing I knew they were putting my sister and me into the car. Well, I didn't want to leave my family so I started crying and screaming. Sis was too young to realize what was happening and seemed excited about going for a ride. They finally took me out of the car and left with her. I remember watching her drive off, banging on the window and crying. I started to get a sick feeling, first my mother and now my sister;

everyone I loved was leaving me. It made me want to crawl deeper into that shell, fetal position, where no one could find me or hurt me anymore.

Two weeks later we got another visit. This time it was another white lady named Ila Hebert, from Baraga, MI. She was somewhat of an intimidating woman because of her large stature. She stood about 5'10" and must have weighed over 200 pounds. She had dark circles under her eyes and had curly, permed hair. She had a kind and generous nature to her personality though, real salt of the earth. She was the type of person that would have helped anyone if she could.

Ila's maiden name was Brownell, and she had a history with Watersmeet, being that three of her brother's lived there. Ila's husband, Bart, was a cousin to Rose. Rose told Ila and Bart about getting my sister as a foster child and that there was still one girl left there. She probably also told them that my dad could be easily persuaded to give me up, too.

The Hebert's had been married for a while but couldn't have children. Ila had lost a daughter, from a previous marriage, when the girl was six years old. There had been something wrong with her heart. Coincidentally, the girl passed away when she was six, the same age as I was when Ila came to get me.

She came, bringing beer, and convinced my dad that I would be better off with them. They had a decent income that would enable them to give me anything I needed. I had a much better attitude then, when I heard I would be in the same town as my sister and that I would be able to see her. Ila and Rose probably told my dad that he could see us once in awhile. With some hesitation, he finally resigned himself to the fact that they were probably right. They told me to go and get my belongings. I came back with a rolled up paper bag, the typical Indian suitcase, that held all of my worldly possessions. I really think that our dad thought it was going to be a temporary situation. Besides, he still had his sons. The distance to Baraga was closer than Harbor Springs so a visit would not be as difficult.

When we arrived in Baraga, it was nighttime, and the first time I had ever seen city lights. I should say village lights. Watersmeet had a population of about 600 or so, and Baraga had a population twice that. There weren't any streetlights where we had lived outside of Watersmeet. When the sun went down it was pitch black outside. You couldn't see your hand in front of your face. Coming down M-38 into Baraga, the highway into town, we crested a hill, and all you could see were the lights of Baraga. The lights of L'Anse, twinkled across the bay of Lake Superior, as they reflected off the lake. I asked if those were stars shining. My new mom laughed and said no, they were streetlights.

Their home was on the main street of town. Downstairs of the building was a restaurant that they owned, and they lived in a large apartment upstairs. My new father lifted me up and showed me around the restaurant that night. The kitchen was located in the back. Out front, there was a large counter with stools, tables and chairs, pinball machines, and a jukebox. The bathroom was also toward the back and a small storage room that later would be a playroom for me.

As he showed me around, I couldn't believe all of the scrumptious-looking food I was seeing. Doughnuts, pies, cakes, candy, and potato chips were stacked up on display cased in glass. I had never tasted or even set my eyes on some of these items. He said, "Are you hungry? What would you like to eat? You can have anything you want!" I answered right away, "potato chips!" He noticed that my little lips were very chapped and cracked. "They'll burn your lips, honey." "I don't care, I still want potato chips!," I answered. I remembered the salty taste that stayed on my tongue the one other time I had them. I just loved the taste of potato chips.

One day, I was playing in front of their house when I spotted some potato chips someone had dropped on the sidewalk. I picked them up, brushed the dirt off, and started eating them. They were horrified when they caught me eating off the ground and quickly told me that it would make me sick. Drinking a pop, too, was a new experience and a real treat for me. We had never had anything but wild meat, things that grew in the woods, or the bland slop they called food at the Harbor Springs School.

The next day they took my little paper bag and tossed it right into the garbage can. There was a little shoe store next door that also had a small clothing line. They bought me new shoes and clothes. I actually had my first pair of pajamas, my own bed with sheets, and warm, clean blankets. They were amazed when I made my own bed, without a wrinkle in it, without being told.

It took some getting use to... all of this attention. It wasn't long after that, they brought me to the doctor in L'Anse for a medical exam. I was 6 years old but only weighed 38 pounds. The doctor said I was malnourished, underweight, and prescribed some vitamins. He observed my walk that was very pigeon-toed and referred me to a specialist. The foot specialist fitted me with very ugly, corrective shoes. He also gave me foot exercises to do every day. This included ten minutes of walking on my tippy toes back and forth, 10 minutes of walking on my heels, then ten minutes of walking on the insides of my feet. I was so self-conscious of the ugly shoes that I would try to hide my feet under my desk at school. It took a few years, but my feet and walk straightened out.

My hair had grown down to my butt. It was thick and heavy, and I started to get headaches. They thought it was from the weight of my hair. My adopted mother had a friend that cut hair. She came over and chopped it all off into a pixie cut. My adopted mother was an excellent cook, and it did not take long for me to gain weight and start looking healthier.

I was able to keep my long hair when I had attended Harbor even after most of the other girls and boys had their long braids severed by the nuns. What better way to strip them of their identity? My father's only request to the priest, when he took us was that they didn't cut my hair. He told him I had better come home with long hair. Natives took pride in their long hair. It was a symbol of the strength of your spirit. Knowing my father, he probably threatened them that if they did cut my hair, he would come down there and burn the place to the ground.

Long hair has tribal religious meaning and the only time it is to be cut is when you are in mourning. It symbolizes the loss of part of self. I feel compelled to share an interesting article that I read on the Internet concerning Natives and their long hair. A woman's husband, who was a psychologist in a Veteran's Administration facility, told her the fascinating, declassified account, of what the U.S. military discovered while recruiting Native Americans for covert actions during the Viet Nam War. They sought out the stealthiest trackers with the keenest senses from the reservations. Before they were put in the field they were given a military haircut. It was determined that they were unable to perform to the same high standard previous to their hair being cut. They then did a study following the trackers. Half of the Native recruits had their hair cut and the other half did not. They set up the scenario to have an enemy creep on both trackers while they slept. The one with his hair cut slept right through the exercise and was captured. The one who did not have his hair cut, awoke, and was able to escape. The belief is that the hair emits energy and serves as a sixth sense. Therefore we are more perceptive of our surroundings. My adopted parents had no knowledge of our cultural values, beliefs, or customs and did not hesitate to have it cut.

I still remember the date Ila came to get me, it was August 2, 1965. I was 6 years old and turning 7, about 2 months later. Like I said, I never had a birthday party, but when my birthday came that year, it was very different. I had cake, balloons, and presents, but I didn't have any friends or family. The Hebert's nieces and girls from down the street that they knew were invited to my party. I was pretty excited but kind of embarrassed by all of the attention. I was not familiar with people being so nice to me and wondered when they were going to start being cruel.

The Hebert's bathroom was being remodeled so they took me out to Mansfieldt's, where my sister was staying, to give me a bath. I had never seen a bathtub before. We were usually scrubbed up in a round washtub or in the rivers. They took my clothes off, filled the tub, and started to coax me into the tub, dragging me by my arms. I was terrified and started screaming. The large, round porcelain tub looked like the water was over my head. I screamed at them, "You're not getting me in that thing!" Once I was immersed in the warm, sudsy water, it felt good, and I learned to like it. That made them chuckle once again.

Ila's half-sister, Francis, lived with them. She was an older woman, totally blind with sunken eyes. She had greying hair and was round in build. Actually, she had one glass eye that she didn't wear often. The other eye didn't have a nerve in it, so it kind of moved around her eyeball socket continuously. I was kind of scared when I looked at her. She also had the bad habit of poking her finger into her eye and keeping it there. That sent shivers down my spine even more.

The Lion's Club had gotten a german-shephard guide dog for her. At first I was frightened by the dog, Misty, who seemed to be bigger than me. The dog was tied in the corner of her bedroom. She never barked or growled, and I grew to like Misty. Francis had been sent to a blind school and got around well for not having sight. Everyday she put the harness on Misty and took her out walking. The dog was very well trained and lead her around to the nearby store, post office, or wherever she needed to go.

Francis loved country/western music. She would sit in her room, rocking in her chair, chain-smoking, and listen to her music for hours on end. She would stack on the LP's or 45's and play one after the other. Her IQ wasn't that high though, she seemed to have the maturity level of a child. She absolutely resented me coming to live with them. She was use to getting all of the attention. When I came, she was jealous and treated me badly. She was giving me a bath one time, stuck my head under the faucet to wash my hair, and used scalding hot water. Of course, I cried. She knew what she was doing and lied when I tried to tell my adopted mother what she had done.

I was told to call her Aunt Francis. Every chance she got she would do or say something evil and hurtful to me. I remember the Wizard of Oz was going to be coming on television. My new mother would be gone to bingo, dad was gone to the bar, and so Francis was left to babysit. I asked my mother if I could watch the show. She said yes, I know my aunt heard her. When it came 8:00 p.m., my normal bedtime, she made me go to bed and wouldn't let me watch it. I cried myself to sleep that night too. She would often tell me, "Why don't you go back to your own kind, where you belong?"

I didn't like looking at her and wished she would wear sunglasses to cover those sunken eyes, but she wouldn't. Later when my sister came to live with us, we took turns leading her around when she went to the doctor's, went up to receive communion at church, or went into the store. Of course, people would stare hard like she was a freak. She would hang on to our arm. We would have to make sure she didn't walk into something. It was very embarrassing when people stared. They would look at her then look at us with pity. I cringed every time we had to take her somewhere.

In spite of my adopted dad being an alcoholic, he never missed a day of work. But he never missed a day of drinking either. Bart, as everyone called him, rather than Bartholomew, was a veteran from WWII and one of his favorite bars was the American Legion bar, a block from the house. He was a taller man, average build, and wore glasses. He always wore his hair in a crewcut. He worked at Pettibone, the main industry in town. They built industrial carry-lifts. It was like a modified tractor, skidder, with hydraulic forks. Mr. LaTendresse, from town, had designed the machine. When they built a new elementary school in Baraga, it was named after him.

Bart also had a part-time job at the post office, which was next door, as the janitor. With their income from the restaurant, caring for the invalid sister, and 2 jobs, their income was middle-class, and we lived a cushy life. Bart always drove a new Dodge truck and Ila always drove new Ford cars. They traded their vehicles in every two years on a new model. They also had nice furniture that certainly didn't come from the dump.

My adopted mother was not a drinker but her vice was bingo. She went just about every night of the week, sometimes even going out of town. My dad would be gone to the bar, and she'd be gone to bingo, so the blind Aunt would babysit me quite often. Mom would bitch about all of the money he spent on beer and he would bitch about how much money she spent on bingo. They would argue and say, "Oh, go have a beer," and the other would say, "Oh, go play with a bingo chip."

They were in their late 30's when I came to live with them. All of the other children my age had parents that were in their twenties. With the age gap, they tended to be old-fashioned and dressed me like I was a little old lady. My dresses were down to the knee or longer while the other girls at school had hip clothes. With my thick, clunky, ugly corrective shoes I had to wear for a number of years, I was a total geek. I took a lot of teasing at school.

All of the other kids had their brothers, sisters, and real parents, but when they asked me questions about my family, I didn't know how to answer. Why did my real parents give me up? Where were my brothers and sisters? I became very shy and didn't like people staring at me. I didn't want to even talk in school. I would try to hide behind the kid who sat in front of me hoping I wouldn't be called on to answer in school.

I remember my first year there. I was going into the 2nd grade. My last name was still Brunk because I wasn't adopted yet. One girl started teasing me on the playground. "Linda Brunk, drunk as a skunk, drunk Brunk," she had all the kids laughing at me. "You better shut-up," I told her. She wouldn't, so I ran over to her, threw her on the ground, jumped on top of her and started banging her head on the ground. That shut her up and she was the one crying then. I had seen enough violence so fighting was nothing new to me. I just did to her what I had seen my dad do to my mom plenty of times. To use someone else's joke, "we learned how to throw a punch from our dad and how to take a punch from our ma."

I liked my second grade teacher. Her name was Miss Hackman, and she was so nice, never raised her voice, what a difference compared to Sister N. I got quite sick during 2nd grade and ended up in the hospital having to get my tonsils and appendics out at the same time. I was there for about two weeks. Miss Hackman had the whole class each make a get-well card for me. My adopted parents brought them to me at the hospital in L'Anse. I cried reading them all because I thought no one liked me the way that they made fun of me. They all wrote that they missed me, they hoped I would get well soon, and couldn't wait to see me again. I eventually made friends with other girls who were teased for being misfits, too.

My first Christmas was unbelievable. I never had toys before. When they asked me what I wanted for Christmas, I didn't know what to say. I had seen toys other kids in the neighborhood played with, and toys that were advertised on this new contraption, called a television. I told them that I thought a bike or doll would be fun to have. My new parents couldn't stand the anticipation, so I was awakened early that morning.

I came around the corner into the living room, still groggy and rubbing my eyes, and squinted at the brightly lit, Christmas tree. Presents were stacked practically to the ceiling, all around the tree, and spewed out into the room. "Look what Santa brought you," they told me excitedly. I was totally speechless as I began ripping into them. I liked this Santa guy. There were dolls, a bike, clothes, books; you name it, and things I never dreamed of having. Their generosity was beyond anything I had ever known. They were spoiling me rotten, and I didn't feel as though I deserved it.

In spite of this new cushy life, I often cried myself to sleep at night, still hurting and aching for my real family. These things were nice enough, but all I wanted was to be back with my real parents, my brothers, and my sisters. I would have given it all up to be back in Watersmeet. I thought that any day now they would be coming for me, and we would be together again. The months began to turn into years of waiting.

I suppose my new parents thought that by giving me things I never had that I would feel loved and special. I was special all right, my adopted dad would soon show me just how special I was to him. He sometimes babysat me, too. He would coax me up on his lap to watch television with him where I would fall asleep in his arms. Then he would carry me into my room and tuck me into bed. I must have slept hard because I would wake up and not remember him carrying me to bed.

I didn't stay a heavy sleeper though. Eventually, I became hypervigilant with my sleep. I would awaken at the slightest stirring. I don't know exactly how old I was, maybe around 8 or 9, when the sexual abuse started. I would just start to doze off in his lap and then he would start to fondle me. It first started on the outside of my clothes and then turned into under my clothes. As his hand slipped up under my pajama top and he began rubbing my chest, it felt kind of soothing. He would do it almost unconsciously while watching television. At that time it almost seemed harmless enough but as I grew older, he still wanted me on his lap, and always seemed to want to be alone with me. He took me for rides with him in the evening on his rounds to the bars.

He had built a camp just outside of town. One day we got a flat tire on the way out there and he stopped to change it. I had my head out the window watching him. I asked him why couldn't just put the flat part up on top. He laughed and said that wouldn't work. As he jacked it up, I said, "Look it isn't flat anymore." More and more he wanted his "new" daughter with him. Wouldn't you think most men would want to spend quality time with their wife rather than their daughter? I didn't understand why he didn't want to be alone with her out there. She was glad I went because she could go to bingo without him complaining.

Baraga Area Schools had older school buildings that were scattered in the township boundaries, before they built the new one. Our third grade was held out in Keweenaw Bay, about six miles north of Baraga. Our teacher's name was Mrs. Williams. She was younger and prettier than Ms. Hackman. I always loved the way she dressed, so feminine, and she had a flair for fashion. I looked forward to seeing the beautiful dresses and outfits she would wear each day. I also enjoyed her book reading to us in the afternoon. Her voice was clear and spellbinding. My favorite was the story about Old Yeller.

Fourth grade didn't go so well. We were bussed out to Pelkie, about 10 miles west of Baraga. The teacher, Mr. Hoppala, seemed to be on the verge of a nervous breakdown. He was at his wits end with our large class. Each year the kids in my grade seemed to be getting rowdier and more out of control. One day, not too long after the school year had began, one of the kids made him very mad at recess. He picked the boy up and threw him over the chain-link fence. We were all flabbergasted. I told my parents what happened when I got home. It was only a couple of days later they pulled me out of public school and put me in the Catholic school located in L'Anse, 3 miles around the bay. Oh mean nuns, "damn penguins," I thought to myself.

Our teacher was Mrs. Forrest. She wasn't too bad. An older woman, very strict, but she treated everyone fairly. She wasn't afraid to slap your hands with a ruler or pull your ear from behind as she walked around the room, if you weren't paying attention. There were a few Indian kids that attended school there, also. L'Anse and Baraga were within the boundaries of the Keweenaw Bay Indian Reservation. I had made a few friends at the school. A few of the boys that attended there I would see later in high school. They transferred over to the Baraga Area Public School. Similar to Harbor Springs, the L'Anse Catholic school only went up to the 8th grade. It was a big relief to get to go home every day.

The school had a few nuns, one in particular taught piano lessons. My parents thought it would be a good idea to buy me a piano and make me take lessons. Sister Selene taught me for a couple of years and I learned to play a little bit. She was very strict and stern. She would holler at me sometimes and make me cry. It stung when she slapped my hands for playing the wrong note. I guess my feelings got hurt easily. It didn't take much to make me cry. I couldn't understand why adults felt the need to slap, smack, whip, kick, or knock you around all the time. She was constantly telling me to sit up straight while slapping me in the back as I played. I only attended Catholic school there for one year. For the fifth grade they sent me back to public school in Baraga, where a brand new school had finally been completed.

I had my daily routine of practicing the piano for a half-hour every day and then doing my foot exercises for half an hour. The doctor told me to walk with a book on my head to ensure that I would develop good posture. I had to get glasses also in the fifth grade. I was quite the fashion statement with my cat-eye frames, ugly, clunky, thick shoes, and old maid clothes. I remember some of the boys drew pictures of me with glasses on and taped them to the back wall.

Sometimes I dreaded going to school expecting that someone would tease me about something. I knew my shoes were not "cool" like the shoes everyone else wore. They had comfortable tennis shoes or go-go looking boots. I remember I had hairy little arms too. Catholic school required all the girls to wear a uniform, jumper-skirt with a white blouse underneath. I always wanted long sleeves so the kids wouldn't make fun of my hairy arms or I'd wear a sweater if my blouse had short sleeves. One time I took a pair of scissors and cut all the hair off my arms. For some reason, it never did grow back. To this day I still don't have any hair on my arms.

Indians have very little body hair anyway. You do not see many Indian men with a mustache or beard unless they have very little Indian blood. I remember my real mother use to tell guys about this down in Milwaukee. She would add that she didn't even have any pubic hair. Some actually believed her. She was kind of crazy like that.

The sexual abuse continued while I was in the fourth and fifth grade. Of course as a child, I couldn't possibly understand what was happening. I only knew it was wrong, and I became even more withdrawn. It seemed as though the shame was evident on my face.

It wasn't until years later, through college classes in deviant human behavior, that I was able to understand the minds of very disturbed individuals. More importantly, professional counselors specializing in this field have helped me come to terms with the abuse. It is difficult to find a good doctor but I managed to. Just because a person has a degree or title behind their name, does not necessarily mean that they are good at what they do.

I've learned that there are similar dynamics occurring with those who commit sexual abuse and those perpetrating domestic violence. Charming individuals seek to gain the trust of the innocent so they can manipulate their victims. They take their time, grooming them, appearing to be kind, caring, loving, and seeing to their every need. In return, the victim almost feels obligated to surrender their mind and body. The abuser effortlessly manipulates situations to be alone with the victim. The ultimate goal for them is to get complete control and self-gratification. I feel the abusers must have socio-pathic tendencies because they easily lie their way out of any accusations while putting on an indignant face.

Victims also take on a role, almost like having a split personality, reality versus denial; one must be a good actor. They become very good at hiding the pain and shame of abuse by putting on a fake happy face, while dying on the inside. All anyone wants is to be loved, but the love given is demented. In some ways, this sick love is better than no love at all.

When an individual is powerless to change the situation, all of that disgust, anger, and frustration is turned inward and becomes self-hatred. It feels as though you deserve to be treated badly. It's hard to allow yourself to trust people when so many have hurt you. It makes you callous and cynical about life and leaves you wondering if there is any loving people out there. The longer it goes on, the more traumatic the act performed, the more of a toll it takes on your psyche. Then again, not everyone's threshold for emotional pain is the same.

I finally started to get a bad attitude and began acting out in my teens. My misfit friends and I began smoking cigarettes, developed an interest in boys, trying drugs, and skipping school. I think the acting out was a cry for help. I hoped that by bringing attention to my behavior, the people in authority would scrutinize the family, and somehow uncover the truth and make it stop.

I felt that my body was all I had to offer someone in return for love. They could do anything they wanted to me, why not, everyone else had? I guess I thought that once they got to know me, they would love me, the way I deserved to be loved. I hoped someone would save me from my father. I didn't feel that there was anyone I could talk to about my problems. I didn't trust my friends. I felt they would betray me about my secret. I wanted it to come out but feared what would happen if it did come out.

Consider that sex abuse occurs in 1 out of every 4 girls, and the statistics are just as startling for boys. It's amazing how many people around us, friends and relatives, have been affected, but may be living in denial. It is easier to suppress bad memories. Too ashamed to admit to the truth and concerned about what others would think of them, they just pretend it never happened. It's no wonder that there are so many maladaptive adults who, though apparently functioning, cope with their childhood abuses by manipulating, bullying, or acquiescing to others on a daily basis.

I've found myself being drawn to others, male or female, with similar personalities and backgrounds. So many of them along the way have shared that they too were abused. More often than not, it was by relatives rather than strangers. But I digress from my story.

Up until the fourth grade, things were tolerable, living with my new family. I had adjusted to my new surroundings again. I still cried myself to sleep many, many nights. I ached for my real parents to get back together and come and get us kids so that we could all be a family once again. I looked forward to my visits with my sister out on the farm. It brought me so much happiness having her close by. We had a lot of fun together playing with all of our new toys. Her foster parents were treating her very badly, though. She told me stories of how Rose would blindfold her and tie her hands behind her back to force-feed her at times. They had a playroom in their farmhouse where Rose would lock my sis and the other foster kids in for most of the day.

Sis was so accident-prone, and I seemed to get caught up in it or blamed for it, somehow. For example, I had a new baby buggy for my dolls that my parents bought me. She was over visiting and wanted to push it down the street. I told her, "Sure, just be careful with it." She took off running with it and hit a crack in the sidewalk that was sticking up high and the wheels broke off. I got my ass chewed off over that.

Another time I had a snow globe I really liked. When you shook it, you could see a pretty little town with glittery snow falling down in it. "Can I play with it," she asked. I said, "Ya, just don't break it." She started to shake it hard, and it slipped out of her hand, hit the floor, and broke. I was starting to think that maybe I should have been telling her to go ahead and break it, then my things wouldn't have gotten broke.

Once our brother made me a miniature bow and arrow that really worked. She wanted to try that, too. She pulled on it too hard, and snapped it in half. I always cried when she broke something of mine because I thought my new parents would get mad at me for not taking better care of my things.

I couldn't stay mad at her though, because, like the things she broke, we had that in common: we were broken, too. However, the bow and arrow was the only thing I had from Luther, and I had cherished it dearly.

A neighborhood friend was teaching me how to ride my new bike. I could balance and steer the bike but hadn't quite mastered using the brake at the same time. She gave me a little push down a little hill that Y'd off at the bottom. She kept yelling for me to turn at the bottom, and I yelled back, "I can't." There was a rose bush in the middle, and I crashed right into it and got all scratched up from the thorns. She was laughing her ass off.

When we were a little older, I spent a night at sis's new home. I was still not too experienced at riding bikes. She was about to have a similar accident, only worse. There was a very steep hill by the house and we were told not to ride down it. Well, we snuck out early in the morning while everyone was still sleeping. We pushed our bikes to the top of the hill. I went down first and made the sharp turn at the bottom, avoiding the barbed-wired fence at the bottom. Then it was sis's turn. As she neared the bottom, I yelled for her to start turning. She hadn't applied the brakes hard enough. "I can't," she yelled. Sure enough, she ran smack dab into that fence. Somehow her leg was all tangled up in the barbed-wire. There was no way of pulling it out without ripping the skin. She was screaming and bleeding profusely. I ran to wake up Uncle Carl, Rose's husband.

Carl was the complete opposite of Rose. He was a very compassionate and kind man. I had never seen him mad. He was a very hard worker. He was usually busy doing farm chores, and we didn't see much of him. I told him what happened. He grabbed a pair of wire cutters and ran out to her. He cut enough of the wire to get her leg out. They wrapped it and rushed her to the hospital to get stitched up. She has scars on her leg from that ordeal. Needless to say, I was grounded for some time for that stunt. I was grounded quite often over things usually having to do with her, come to think of it.

I wasn't use to being around farm animals, and some of Uncle Carl's animals scared me. They had geese and goats that use to chase after us and bite us. Once, we were looking for Uncle Carl, and figured he was probably milking the cows in the barn. I opened up the heavy barn door only to see a huge bull standing there. His head was as big as I was, and his two, long horns were pointing directly at me. He stood about two feet in front of us, staring, as if he was about to charge. He was probably too big to even fit through the door, but I wasn't taking any chances. I slammed the door shut as fast as I could while sis stood there laughing wildly.

Maybe about four or five times while growing up in Baraga, our real father came to visit. On one of those visits, he brought our brothers along. It was usually a short half-hour visit or so. They stopped by to see sis first. She told me that she could see them coming way down the dusty dirt road to the farm. She was going to surprise them on the corner. She ducked down in the long grass to hide. It just so happened there was a big mud-puddle on the same corner. They drove through it and splashed the puddle all over her. Like I said, trouble had a habit of following her.

My adopted mother picked up my sis to come with us to have a meeting of sorts with our birth mother. I must have been about 9 or 10, shortly before they officially adopted me. We met out at the park at Bass Lake near Watersmeet. They sat at a picnic table and talked. Sis and I played with our younger sister on the swings. It was the first time we had seen her since she was a baby. By then she was about 2 or 3. She had dark hair and eyes like me but her face and mouth looked like sis. I remember we were telling each other, "She looks like me." "No, she don't, she looks like me," we both laughed. Actually, she looked like both of us.

Apparently, what I could glean from that meeting, our real mother told our new mom that she would not interfere in our life or try to get us back. She explained why she had left and agreed that we would have a better life in Baraga than what she could give us. That was the last we saw of our mother and our youngest sister. There were no phone calls or letters either.

By then it didn't hurt quite as bad as the first time she left. Maybe it was all the new toys and friends we had, or maybe it was not seeing her for so many years, or maybe I just didn't care anymore.

FAMILY FRIEND WITH BENEFITS

Father Christopher was a short man with a goatee. He dressed in the long brown robe that monks wear with a white rope belted at the waist. He was the pastor in Zeba, north of L'Anse, where many natives attended the small church. He was also one of the same priests that drove Indian children down to Harbor Springs. The Hebert's were also Catholic, so I assume that was the connection of how he became a family friend with them. My mother invited him over for dinner every Saturday evening. I think she thought it was somewhat prestigious to have a religious man in their circle of friends.

She would set the table more formally, and dinner would include the main course, salad, and a dessert. There is no doubt the woman was an excellent cook. It came from many years of experience of caring for her younger brothers and sisters after her parents died at a young age. My adopted parents both, as with many from that generation, dropped out of school in the 8th grade to take on adult responsibilities at home.

Fr. Christopher's rectory was a trailer located just down from the church. He must have asked for help with chores around the church and rectory, cleaning, putting together the bulletin, or to keep him company on his trips around the area to other parishes. Ila decided to send me to accompany him, thinking I was certainly in safe company.

We attended church in Baraga, at St. Ann's, but attended catechism in Zeba, at Fr. Christopher's church once a week. I met other native girls from Zeba and the Baraga side that also went to religion classes there. We were all close in age. I noticed Father Christopher coming up behind the girls, hugging them tightly and then rubbing his hands up and down on their newly developing chests. I could tell they were as uncomfortable as I was when he did that.

I usually was one of the last kids hanging around waiting for him to give me a ride home. He would tell me to lay down and take a nap while he finished up and he would wake me when it was time to go. I was awakened to him rubbing his hand on my crotch on the outside of my pants. "Time to go," he told me. On the ride home he would slide his hand up and down on my leg. This happened often when I accompanied him on rides. I tried not to fall asleep because his hand would be where it shouldn't be when I woke. It was hard staying awake, with the warm sun shining on me through the window, and lack of sleep from restless nights.

Most of the time I would pretend I was sleeping, just like I did when my dad did the same thing to me. What was wrong with these people? Maybe this is what all girls go through. This is how men treat girls when no one was around. Not only girls, but boys, too, after what I learned happened at Harbor Springs. It's as if being sexually abused was our rite of passage. It is such a taboo subject, not only in the U.S. but all over the world. No one wants to discuss it or deal with this issue, as prevalent as it is. It may even be acceptable in some cultures, who knows.

This priest molested me on many occasions. From what I observed, it looked like he was molesting other girls, too. Whether he put his hands on the altar boys that way, I'm not sure, but I know now that usually there is never just one victim, but many. These pedophiles are very good at getting themselves around children and are good at convincing people of their "saintly" nature.

It makes me sick. Sometimes I think they should all be rounded up and have done to them the same horrific crimes they've committed against the innocent. They should have their nipples put in a vice and twisted until they are pulled right off. Then they should be raped up the ass with a baseball bat until they pass out. Then they should have the bat pulled out of their ass and rammed down their throat. Maybe then they would understand what it feels like to be victimized, traumatized, and violated. They should have this done to them as many times as they did it to someone else. I'm not serious, I'm just saying .. Fantasies of revenge are a normal reaction to abuse.

I wouldn't want to do it or watch it be done to anyone else. I was trying to put the scenario into a perspective that equaled the pain. What would be a just punishment? I think I developed the Stockholm syndrome. I pity the perpetrators because I realize they probably had something awful done to them also that turned them into such animals. I feel as though I could endure more emotional pain than they could, having gone through it so often and for so long.

Father Christopher continued to come over for dinner, I was sent to help him at the rectory, and he continued to try and feel me up. Not too long after that though we got news that he was killed in a car accident. I kind of thought, maybe that was God's way of punishing him or making the abuse stop. He probably knew I could only handle so much, and He was right. I couldn't speak of what my adopted dad was doing and I sure as heck wasn't going to tell anyone what this priest was doing. Besides who would believe a kid over an adult or a priest?

You know how they say, everything happens for a reason? I just couldn't wrap my head around why this was happening to me. Was I really that worthless that I deserved such treatment? Was that all I was good for? I guess it was part of life. You have to learn to take the bad with the good. I was as helpless to do anything about the situation as my birth parents were when we were taken from them or sent to Harbor Springs.

Later, Father Christopher was replaced with another priest named Father Elmer. I had heard stories when I got older from girls that went to catechism there too. One girl said her mother use to be drunk all the time and would send her and her sister's over to the rectory to help out with tasks around the church. Father Elmer had picked up where Father Christopher left off. She said he would actually give the girls a bath in his tub, get naked with them and have them sit on him. I can only imagine what else he did to them.

These men of God take an oath of celibacy but break their vows when they molest, fondle, and rape innocent children. A lot of altar boys have gone through the same horrors. All of the incidents in the news of similar cases all end in the same way. They transfer these pedophiles to another parish where they can do it again. Anyone else in the mainstream would be sent to prison, why do we never hear of criminal prosecutions of priests? The Church doesn't even seem to address the issue, advocate for the victims, pursue investigations, or try to make amends.

My adopted parents never took any money or assistance from the state for my care. Before they legally adopted me I was considered a ward of the state. There was a man named Mr. Dault, who was the county probation officer but was also tasked with "checking" on me. He was a white man, very tall, good-looking, and seemed so kind and soft-spoken. He made periodic visits to our house and spoke with me in private. I liked him and wanted so bad to tell him the truth. He asked how things were going and if I liked my new family. I was too young to put into words what was going on. I was also too scared of what would happen if I did tell on these adults. I somehow knew they would be in a lot of trouble, and I didn't want to be the cause of it. I certainly did not want to be blamed for it either.

I felt strongly that they just would not believe me, a child over the priest, God's right arm man. Would they believe the child over the adult who has taken her in and given her a better life? Mr. Dault had a gentle way about him, but it was almost as if he was expecting to hear something warm and fuzzy. I always told him, without looking him in the eye, that everything was good.

That is a trait of native people though, too, they do not believe in looking someone directly in the eyes, out of respect. They believe to hold direct eye contact for too long is a sign of aggression. That is how I was raised and later in life, I had to make a conscious effort to make eye contact while talking to people. Non-Indians usually see this as a sign that the person must be shifty or shady. Our comfort zone, or personal space, also seemed to be a little bigger than the non-Indians are. I don't care for someone all up in my face, feeling their breath on me, or close enough to be touching me when you are trying to talk to them.

I just couldn't bring myself to say what needed to be said when being questioned by Mr. Dault. The secret was never spoken about. The abusers never had to tell me not to say anything, I just somehow knew better. Besides that, I didn't want to be ripped away from the only real family I had left, my sister. If I was removed from this home, it might be to a different town where I wouldn't be close to her. The next family or placement might even be worse, if that was possible. I didn't want to be away from sis ever again. I knew she needed me, and I needed her. We weren't living in the same household, yet.

ANOTHER DAY, ANOTHER VICTIM

There were some major changes coming when I was in the 6th grade. I was changing into a young woman and had my first moon in the 6th grade. My new mother explained to me how to deal with it and what it meant. We had the sex education talk in school the previous year so I knew what to expect. The boob-fairy came to visit me that year. This was somewhat early; not too many other girls developed this early. The thought of it all frightened me, but now I had an excuse, I thought my dad would be leaving me alone more now.

My parents sold their house downtown and bought a small house near the school. The blind, evil aunt was still living with us and being a bitch. She did what she could to get my parents mad at me. If she told them I sassed her I would be grounded and couldn't leave the house.

My dad's camp was outside of town about six or seven miles. He would drive out there almost nightly to check on it and usually had me go with him. Camps were really big in the U.P. They were usually shacks, but were places where people could get out of town and party more privately. They were usually used for a place to stay while they went out hunting, too. He had gaslights run by a generator and heated the place with a woodstove. This is where he kept a lot of his smut books. This was also the hell-house where most of the abuse took place. It was also the place where he would tear the copper wires out of small motors. He would burn the copper down and turn it in for beer money.

This was the same year that the Mansfeldt's quit taking in foster kids, which was probably a good thing. Sis was going to have to either go back to Harbor Springs or be sent to another foster family, which could have been out of the area. When I was told this, I begged the Hebert's to let her come and

61

live with us. I promised she wouldn't be any trouble, and that I would take care of her and watch out for her all of the time. She didn't want to go back to Harbor Springs. She said she thought the nuns were trying to kill her.

She told me a story about Halloween down there. She said that they had the bottom floor all decorated spooky and scary. She said they had the kids bobbing for apples and when she bobbed for an apple, someone held her head under water, and she thought she was going to drown. Then she said when she came around a corner, still wet from that, someone hit her in the face with a big powder puff and almost choked her with the powder.

By then the Hebert's had officially adopted me. I was no longer Linda Raye Brunk. I was now Linda Raye Hebert. They agreed to take in sis and soon adopted her, too.

I remember how it all came about. Sis was over visiting us one day. My mother was sitting on the couch playing bingo, which at that time was on television. Sis and I were lying on the floor playing with something. Ila started grilling her, "Do you like living at Mansfeldt's?" She looked at me, probably more for comfort- -we had a knowing look we gave each other—then answered her, "Yes." "Do you like living in Baraga?" She glanced at me again, and I looked at her waiting for her to answer. "Yes," she said. "Do you think you'd want to come and live with us?" she asked. Sis looked at me, and my eyes got big, and I nodded my head yes, and she said, "Yes!" At that, my mother's big frame put her bingo cards down, and she started to get up. "What are you going to do, Aunt Ila?" she asked. "I'm going to give Linda a spanking for telling you what to say." I didn't care as long as my sister got to come and live with us.

Now I had someone to go out to the camp from hell with, but that was where all the fun was, too. Bart bought us a mini-bike but we could only ride it out to camp. They bought two snowmobiles, but if we wanted to ride them, we had to go to camp. That was where, if we wanted to learn how to drive a stick-shift, we would have to go practice on the back roads with him. If we wanted to sneak a cigarette, he would let us do it out at camp. If we wanted to try a beer, he would give it to us out at camp. There were lots of secrets to keep.

Bart's brother had a camp right next to his. They had a big family with two girls our age, so we often played with them out to camp. Our adopted relatives always treated us as if we were related by blood. There were a few occasions that I had cousins or a friend sleep over out there. I suspect he creeped over to their bed in the middle of the night. I tried not to think about it. Nothing was ever said between any of us concerning that topic.

Our parents were constantly telling us what lowlife's our real parents were. My mother, they said, had lots of boyfriends, and my dad was nothing but a drunk. They would ask us, "How could parents think more of themselves and nothing for their own children." They tried to put our biological family in the worst light. They probably thought we would be more grateful for what we had now and had to remind us just how bad off we would be if we were still with them.

It was during this time that my real dad's brother, Uncle Albert and his family, moved to Baraga. Actually, our adopted dad helped him get a job at Pettibone. Finally, we had a touch of home, a connection to our blood, our cousins to hang with. We had two Aunt Betty's. My mother's sister's name was Betty, also. My father would come up to see his brother and sister-in-law and stop by briefly to see us. It was not very often because he did not have the money or a ride up to Baraga. However, our brothers, Luther and Melvin came often, usually by hitch-hiking. Even though Uncle Albert and Aunt Betty had 8 kids of their own, they never gave it a second thought whether Luther and Melvin could stay with them.

This Aunt Betty made the best fried-bread we ever ate. It was a real treat! Our cousins would let us know they were up and we would sneak over there to visit the boys. Sometimes they stopped by the house to see us when we were home alone. Usually our adopted dad was gone to the bar and mother was gone to bingo. They usually dropped the blind, bitch aunt off to visit one of their relatives.

True to my word, my sister was with me everywhere I went. She tagged along as if she were my shadow. I was old enough to babysit, and we would stay home, watch television, ride our bikes, go to the playground next to our house, or play in our bedroom. We also had gotten cassette players for Christmas. We would tape ourselves singing, telling jokes, or farting into the microphone. We'd then play it back and crack-up laughing.

Once we slid the player, turned the recorder on, into our Aunt Francis' room. We knew we could eventually get her swearing because she cussed like a pirate. We never swore, of course. They thought "shit" was a swear word. We heard her drop something, and she yelled, "Goddamn it!" We pulled it back out of her room. Then when our parents were home, we rewound it and turned it up loud, "Goddamn it!" Our mother said, "Hey, who's swearing in there?" We told her what we did. She laughed! But said not to do it again and that she had better not ever catch us using that language.

We listened, of course, because we never disobeyed or talked back. She always threatened that she would "knock our teeth down our throat," if we "got smart with her". If we dared to roll our eyes at her, she would say, "don't roll your eyes at me or I'll roll them right out of the back of your head." The threats were enough to make us tow the line because we knew she was big enough to do it. When she yelled it practically blew your hair back.

I remember one time when our mother was in the hospital, our dad had a few beers at the house and talked Aunt Francis into having a few with him. She had gotten a buzz-on, so he put her to bed and was in her room for quite a while. El- sicko. We thought, better her than us.

Sis and I had a double-bed we shared. When we slept together we were always tightly wrapped around each other, symbolically never wanting to let go of each other or be separated ever again. Eventually, we got bunkbeds. I always slept on the top and she slept on the bottom bunk. One time we decided to switch beds. When our alarm went off the next morning for school, we both jumped up. I was thinking I was still on the top and sat up real quick. My hair got caught in the springs under the top bed. She was thinking she was still on the bottom and swung her legs over the side to stand up. She fell and hit the floor. We both got scuffed up but laughed and laughed at what had happened. She used to like it when I laid on the bottom. She would lie on the top bunk, and I would take both feet and push up on the mattress and bounce her. If I went to visit friends she came with me. We were inseparable. We attended the local basketball and football games together.

Our brothers were at the age they started to get into trouble, smoking, drinking, chasing girls, skipping school, etc. They often hitch-hiked all the way to Milwaukee to stay with our mom and then hitch-hiked back to Watersmeet where our dad still lived. When they came to town, it felt like the good 'ol days back in Watersmeet. Our cousins were rough-necks and always had our back. They were scrappers, too. I guess you could say we all were. We had witnessed enough violence in our young life. The Indian girls from Watersmeet never hesitated to throw down when someone really pissed us off. If they witnessed you getting picked on, they would dare you, "are you going to take that shit?"

Although we didn't get to see our real parents as much as we would have liked, it was so awesome seeing our brothers. They were good-looking boys and would crack everyone up with their wit, pranks, and jokes. They had a way of ripping on everyone and everything. We always had a good time being around them. We missed them and loved them so much. Sis and I could only imagine what it would have been like to have our brothers around all of the time to protect us and have fun with. We just couldn't find the courage to tell them either about what was going on.

Our adopted parents must not have had a sex life. We could never hear anything sexually going on through the walls. They usually slept with their bedroom door open. That is probably why he turned to me and eventually my sister for his jollies or to get his rocks off. We were usually forced to go out to camp with Bart. "Oh, go keep your dad company," our mother would tell us. We would actually get grounded if we didn't want to go with him. They would tell us, "Well, then don't ask to go anywhere else either." There is no way she could not have known what was going on. She had to have seen the devastated look on my face coming home after a night with him. My stomach would just churn when the weekends came up, and he talked about wanting to spend a night out there. She didn't mind him going because he wouldn't be nagging her for sex.

There were two double beds out at the camp. Before sis came he usually carried me to his bed in the middle of the night or put a pillow in between us. If and when he woke me by touching me, I would start crying and tell him to stop or leave me alone. He usually did. When sis came, we slept together in the other bed. He would tell us to make sure we wore a nightgown because it got hot in the camp with the wood heat. And, of course, nightgowns were easier to slide up. "Don't wear underwear, it's not healthy for you," he would tell us. Well, we would wear underwear, pajamas with the legs, and our housecoat buttoned up to our neck. Then we pulled the blankets up, wrapped our arms around each other, and tucked the blankets under each other's legs. We would be sweating our asses off but at least would wake up when he started trying to uncover us. He was usually in a stupor from drinking, we would yell at him to quit, leave us alone, and he would stagger back to his bed.

When sis first came and he made us sleep with him, I would just lie there quietly so she wouldn't wake and be scared. I let him touch me. He would get his little thrill then go back to sleep. I figured I was use to it happening already for years and maybe he would leave her alone. It wasn't long before he was trying to make his move on her. She was always more bold than me. She was three years younger, but I admired her bravery. She would really yell at him and say, "Leave her alone!" Or, "what are you doing?" He would back off then. I always cried after it happened. More often he would only take me out to camp while sis stayed home. I preferred the abuse happen to me rather than her. I didn't want her to suffer any more than she had to.

Even at home when it didn't happen, I cried myself to sleep wondering when was it going to stop. Why wouldn't God stop it, why wouldn't my parents come and get me? I wondered how much worse could it get. How would I ever get through it without losing my mind? I learned how to cry without making a peep. It was like down in Harbor Springs, crying silently in the dark. I didn't want my mother to come in my room and ask what was wrong or why was I crying. I figured she wouldn't believe the awful thing her husband was doing anyway. I just let the tears stream down my face and licked the salty taste off when they hit my lips as I laid there holding myself.

The Catholic Church was only a couple of blocks from our house. Our parents quit going but sis and I were both required attending mass on a weekly basis. The priest's name was Fr. Oremus. One day, he was talking to us about being adopted and how special that made us. He told us that any time we wanted to talk about anything, he would be there for us, we could come and see him. We were working up our nerve to go and see him and tell him about the abuse that was going on. Before we could get over there, he too, was killed in a car accident.

The new priest that replaced him didn't seem as friendly and compassionate. We thought we would try to approach him anyway. We sneaked over to the rectory, knocked on the door, and he told us to come in. I don't remember the exact words I used, but I tried to explain that our dad was touching us in a way that we didn't like. I also said that this family wasn't our real family and we didn't want to live there anymore. His reaction was not what we had expected. He seemed somewhat shocked and told us that we had better go back home and be thankful and honor our parents. At that point, we became fearful that our parents would find out what we had done. We dared not try again to tell anyone. We saw where that got us.

I was getting older, he was getting bolder, my mind was not my own anymore. I felt numbed out from everything. I would have to space out, pretend it wasn't really happening, and just wait for the day that I would turn 18. I couldn't wait until I had a boyfriend, maybe he would save me, take me away from that hellhouse.

Our mother got us diaries one year for Christmas. I enjoyed expressing my thoughts on paper. Sometimes I would write about sis and me sneaking out of the game to go riding around with boys. Sometimes I would write about our dad touching me and how much I hated it. I would write that part sloppy so you couldn't really make it out, but I knew what it said. I don't remember where I use to hide it, maybe under my mattress. One day I came home from school, I had butterflies in my stomach, almost like intuition or instinct of an impending doom. I walked in the house and my mother said one of my aunt's had called her and told her what I had been up to. She told her that she seen us riding around with boys. It was almost word for word what I had written in my diary.

She wanted to know what else we were up to with boys. She gave me a big lecture about kissing boys or letting them touch me. She said that was supposed to be saved for marriage and that no man would ever want a girl who was "dirty" like that. I got grounded, as usual, and never wrote another thing in the diary. That was such a betrayal. Maybe that was her way of trying to get me to talk about what was really going on. But it was done in a manner that sounded more accusatory. Even my own private thoughts were being stolen from me.

I thought to myself that if I weren't such a chicken I would tell her right then and there what was going on. I would hit her right between the eyes with the truth of what her husband was doing to his own daughters. I wanted to tell her if any man was making me dirty, it was her unfaithful husband, and why wasn't she protecting us from him.

They threatened us many times that if we didn't behave they could easily send us away. They said it would most likely be to a detention center where we would be locked up until we turned 18. We wouldn't be sent back to our real parents because they didn't want us anyway, they told us. I believed them. I knew the way we were shuffled around and treated by people that the next place might even be worse.

Aunt Francis often made it a point to try and get us in trouble around the time we wanted to go to a game or a dance so that we would be grounded. They naturally believed her before they would us. When no one was around we would go up behind her and flip her off with both hands, stick our tongue out at her, or make punching and kicking motions in the air at her.

They watched us like a hawk or they had their relatives watching out for us around town. We weren't allowed to do much but sit home. Any misstep and we would get grounded, which meant no basketball games, dances, football games, or sleeping over our friend's house.

I had tried out for cheerleading in the 7th and 8th grade. I had no problem making the squad. I looked forward to getting out of the house and scoping out the boys. I was a late bloomer but boys were starting to take an interest in me. Sis usually went along to the games on the fan bus. She was also in band and played the flute and clarinet. She would play during half-time at the home games.

Any time away from that house made life more bearable. I didn't know it at the time, but given the high statistics for victims of abuse, male and female, there were most likely many in our school too, that I didn't realize were going through the same thing. They always teach kids to be wary of strangers but hardly ever teach you to watch out for grandpa, uncle, cousin, the priest, older sibling, or step-dad.

PUBLIC SCHOOL DAYS

I really enjoyed school. It seemed to be the only time when my life seemed somewhat normal. It was a way to escape from the madness of that house. I always got good grades in my art classes. I was pretty good at gym class, too. I did however, struggle with science, history, and geography. We started physical education in the fifth grade. I loved playing games. It brought back memories of running through the woods as fast as our little legs would carry us. I was built somewhat petite, but I was strong for my size.

One girl I remember from school that stood out from the rest was D. She was very popular in our class. She was a cute little blond haired, blue-eyed thing, and most of the boys seemed to have a crush on her. She was very athletic, also. Year after year, it came down to the two of us being so competitive that our gym teacher usually matched us up as team captains. We would pick our teams, one girl at a time. She picked the most popular girls, and I usually chose the other Indian girls first, whether they were good or not. Even when I wasn't a captain, I was not one of the first ones to be picked for their team, even though I could have been an asset, I wasn't part of their clique. Our competitiveness led to some very good matches and close games. This went on all through high school.

When it came time for the annual strength and stamina testing, it was D. and I who would have the best time, the most sit-ups, push-ups, whatever. When we did the softball throw, the first 8 girls or so, could not throw very far. It seemed liked they were throwing with their left hand. When it was my turn, they would all back up, and my throw usually went over their heads. When we played dodgeball, they could not get me out. I would be the last girl standing. Whatever I did, I did it with all of my might, using every muscle I had, as if running on the paths we made in the woods in Watersmeet. Our school had minimal gymnastic equipment. Having strength and flexibility allowed me to be good at tumbling, flipping, splits, and backbends. Throwing myself into physical challenges brought me joy. It still does. Even as a grandma, I still get out on the lawn and show the grandkids how to do flips, handstands, cartwheels, etc. Sometimes being young at heart and child-like somehow makes up for my lost childhood.

I do not mean to sound like a braggart. Boastfulness is not a characteristic that is looked upon favorably in our culture. Rather, I am acknowledging my strengths and reminding myself that I was good at some things. I worked at keeping my figure as trim as I could. I guess I got that message early. After all, my body was what the opposite sex found attractive. My Catholic upbringing taught us that our body was a temple, take care of it. My parents told us, "if you're going to do something, do it to the very best of your ability." I actually liked exercise, too, every morning I did 50 sit-ups, and every evening 50 sit-ups. I liked the feeling of being strong. It was a way I could burn off excess energy. If need be, maybe the time would come that I would need that strength to help out in some way.

A lot of the girls didn't like me in gym class. They knew if I was throwing the ball at them to get them out, I wouldn't miss, and it was going to leave a mark. My sis was athletic, too. She was always a better ball-player than I was. I tried to teach her to be tough and not to take any crap from anyone. She excelled in that department.

As my figure changed, the boys started to notice me in junior high. It wasn't long before a couple boys left notes in my desk telling me they liked me. I didn't know what to make of it. There was no one in particular that I had a crush on. My friends and I would try to determine who we thought was "the cutest" in our grade. A couple of brave ones called my house to talk to me. I remember one boy from L'Anse that I had met at a football game called the house. My dad answered and told him not to call ever again. He said I wasn't allowed to talk to boys, some he even threatened to call the cops. I was so humiliated. He was so possessive, like I was his private property.

If we weren't stuck at home then we had to go with him. His normal routine was to stop by the camp and then go to the bar. It was usually the bar/bowling alley not far from the camp. We didn't mind because if we weren't bowling we would shoot pool or play fooseball while we waited for him to finish his beer. We played each other and got very good at fooseball. We were so good that we would take on older boys and run the table. It was funny because they thought it wouldn't take long to whoop our butts. They ended up getting spanked by a couple of girls.

Sis and I were rarely ever allowed to go anywhere by ourselves. Most kids our age, went unsupervised, did what they wanted, and didn't have an early curfew like we did. We mostly stayed in the yard. Once we moved up by the school, there were a few neighborhood kids our age to hang out with. Some were boys. We had seen a few of them playing across the way so we went to join them. We didn't care if they were boys; we thought we could give them a run for their money.

They wanted to play football but no one had a football. That's when we remembered our dad had a football that he had gotten from somewhere, maybe an NFL game or something, because it was signed by his favorite team, the Packers. I think he only liked them because the quarterback's name was Bart Starr, the same as his name. That was his handle on the CB radio, too. So we ran home and got that football to use. It was all muddy and ragged up by the time we got done with it. We just left it in the field figuring the boys would get more use out of it than we did. We didn't say anything when our dad asked what happened to it.

We would play croquet and badminton in the yard. To make it more interesting, sis would get in front of the house, and I would get in back of the house. We would bat the birdie back and forth over the house. It was only a one-story house but it was fun. Another thing we use to like to do was lay in the front yard to suntan. We rarely got to go to the lake swimming.

When I got to high school, the football field was practically right next to our house, across a ditch. We would lay out in our bikinis and watch the football players run up on the field for practice. That was fun too because we were getting to be boy crazy. We tried to distract them by rubbing oil all over our brown, half-naked bodies, or squirting each other with the hose and squealing.

My parents did encourage me to start working to earn money as early as I could. I have to say that I did admire their work ethic. My father, even though he was a drunk, worked steadfastly, and our mother always had something going. She ran the restaurant for a number of years. When they closed that, it became an REA station, for freight. The railroad ran right through town and behind the house. She liked to sew and crochet. She was very talented with her hobbies. She made dolls, afghans, etc. and sold them. She would also get lucky at bingo and win big jackpots every now and then.

Her many projects left piles of messes around the house. Our house was not filthy, just very cluttered. We had to thoroughly clean the house every Saturday morning, vacuum, dust the furniture, laundry, dishes, etc. I sometimes thought they only wanted us so we could be their slaves. Sis always volunteered to do the living room. I would go in to check on her only to find her sitting on the floor, dusting the same table over and over while she stared at the cartoons on t.v. I would have to yell at her to get her ass busy or shut the t.v. off. I guess I was pretty bossy.

I started babysitting and started my own bank account. I was only allowed to babysit for my mother's niece, who had 3 kids. She lived close, a couple of blocks away. I managed to save up around $600.00 for my first car in the 10th grade. Our dad had taught me how to drive years before. His truck had a stick-shift too. Learning to operate the clutch and gas simultaneously was tricky. I kept stalling it out. One evening I was waiting outside the bar for him to come out. I wanted to listen to the radio. I leaned over to turn the key and forgot you needed to push in the clutch. The truck jumped forward like a hopping kangaroo. I quickly turned the key off and it stopped inches before smashing into the back of the car parked in front of us.

As a way to entice us to go to camp, he would let us drive his truck.

Naturally, they wouldn't let me take my car and go cruising with it. I was only permitted to run errands for them or give the blind aunt a ride where she needed to go.

They had me buy my own school clothes with the money I had saved. I was finally in style with the rest of the girls. I think I had good taste in fashion. I bought clothes that fit me better than the hand-me-downs and old lady clothes our mother made us wear. I bought clothes that flattered my figure. I wanted to show that I wasn't the dowdy geek everyone thought I was.

The Keweenaw Bay Indian Community reservation was also in Baraga. They instituted youth programs that put the Native teenagers to work on projects around the community during summer vacation. That was where the majority of my savings came from. It was mostly jobs painting, mowing, and picking up garbage, things of that nature. Later in high school, they had internship programs for students, such as clerical jobs in the various departments. You had to be at least 14 years of age. It was something productive to do in the summer and helped kids stay out of trouble. You had to keep your grades up to participate in the internship programs and you could receive credits towards graduation.

The tribe did an excellent job giving kids incentives to stay in school. They held banquets, and gave financial support toward the graduation costs of class pictures, rings, and announcements. They also gave accolades to students that made the honor roll. High school guidance counselors and tutors were provided to those who fell behind. At that time, the dropout rate was high for Indian kids.

Looking back, the tribe was a catalyst in giving our youth opportunities, teaching them to have a work ethic and how to be responsible. They encouraged and supported our youth to go to college and make a better life for themselves. Programs were initiated that allowed students to take field trips and attend summer science camps at the local universities in Houghton and Marquette.

While in school, I made friends with other Native kids that seemed to have a lot in common with me. We all had a good time together. They did a lot of experimenting with drinking, smoking, drugs, and skipping school. Me and my shadow gave in to peer pressure and started becoming sneaky to be part of the crowd. I didn't go out for cheerleading or girls basketball, even though I could have made it. I didn't want my friends to think I was a goody two-shoes. It was bad enough they thought it was weird that we were hardly ever allowed to do anything or stay out late. Our curfew was 9:00 p.m. in high school. We began to forge our parent's handwriting and say that we would not be in school for part of a day due to an appointment. Sometimes we would fake that we were sick. At times we lied and said we were going somewhere but instead sneaked off to meet boys. There were some private out-of-the-way, party places where kids wouldn't be found, usually in the woods.

We were in the 9th grade when we started acting out. My sis learned everything even younger than I did because she tagged along with my friends and me. We threw her a pile of comic books to read while we talked about boys. We discussed who was cute, who was our first kiss, how he kissed, what he tried (with his wandering hands), who we had a crush on, and who had a nice body. They taught me how to french-inhale a cigarette and told me how to give a hickey. The first time I was ever french-kissed was by a boy a year or two older than I was. He came at me with his mouth open so wide I thought he was going to swallow me. Then he stuck his whole tongue down my throat and gagged me. I almost threw up. It was as though I had just got licked in the face by a dog with a big tongue. I wiped it off with my sleeve and thought that was not a pleasant experience. Actually, I thought it was kind of gross.

By then we all had crushes on the same boys, two brothers, who's names started with a D. They had light hair, deep voices, and tattoos on their hands and arms. What was even more appealing was their anti-authority attitude. I kind of admired their rebellious nature and wished I could be more like that. They seemed to do whatever they wanted. Our crowd was starting to smoke pot and do some acid. Those boys did it so, of course, we wanted to try it. We didn't want them to think we were "square." We got pretty ripped up and couldn't stop laughing. These two brothers had two sisters so we told our parents we were going to visit the girls. Their brothers' bedroom was in the basement. They played guitar, sang, and played records by all the popular rock bands. They were exciting to be around compared to the straight-laced life we lived. Their family eventually moved downstate. The brothers left many broken hearts when they left town. My first tattoo was of a cross on my hand that we had seen on their hands. My friends and I all made our own tattoos with India ink and a sewing needle with thread wrapped around it. It also symbolized our Christian upbringing.

One of my girlfriends and I heard the boys were going to be moving, and we wanted to get something of theirs to remember them by. Back then people left their doors unlocked. It was during the summer and their back door, which was a sliding patio door, was wide open. No one was home so we thought we could sneak down in their bedroom and grab a couple of albums that we all liked listening to together. We grabbed a couple and thought we heard someone coming. We went to run back out of the house. We had shut the screen door, but the way the light was reflecting made it look like it was open. My friend, in a panic, was running fast and thought she was going right through it. She hit the screen so hard she bounced right off and landed on her ass. I laughed so hard I thought I was going to pee my pants. Okay, technically, it was more than a prank and could have been construed as breaking and entering, trespassing, and theft.

When our cousins told us that our brothers, Melvin and Luther, would be coming for a visit, we told them that we would meet them downtown. There was a community hill where young people sat and just hung out. They would smoke cigarettes and watch the girls go by or see who was driving down the main street. One of the popular bars was right across the street. It was called the Drift Inn. People would drift in sober and drift out drunk, and it was funny watching them staggering around looking for their cars.

Well, sis and I went down to meet the boys and our cousins on the hill. We were all sitting there, and this one girl named Jean came walking by. The boys had the perfect birds-eye view. They checked her out like guys do, and she knew they were watching her. She was swinging her hips as she strutted down the sidewalk. One of the boys yelled, "Hi Geed!" "Hi!" she yelled back. Everyone just busted out laughing. The first time I ever heard the word "geed,"

I must have been about 5 years old. I remember my real parents fighting, and my dad told my mom that he knew she let some guy named A. play with her geed. I didn't know what that meant at the time. Years later when I was an adult someone told me it is Ojibway, and it means vagina. Jean thought they yelled, "Hi Jean." It was times like that, that made life more bearable, a good laugh with family.

I knew the boys were going through their own hell. I knew they missed their sisters. I knew they missed our real mother. I knew our real dad was probably beating them up. They were acting out doing illegal activities, like stealing cars and committing B&E's. They were on the verge of being sent to jail. I recall my real dad telling me about Luther getting into trouble somewhere, trying to outrun the cops, and they shot up his car. Both of the boys were threatened with some serious prison time and were given the choice of going to jail or joining the service. Of course, they chose the latter, which is probably the best thing that could have happened to them. They went into the service as boys at seventeen and came home as men. They followed in our father's footsteps being very young when going into the service. Melvin enlisted in the Army and Luther became a Marine.

I became aware of some interesting statistics while researching my culture in college. Did you know that on a per capita basis, Natives have a 40% higher voluntary enlistment rate than any other race? In spite of the history of persecution and discrimination, known by many as World War Warriors, they enlisted by the thousands to defend our country. The Navajo code talkers played a major role in winning the war. They were able to relay critical information and the Japanese were unable to translate or break the language. Other native languages were also used including Chippewa and Oneida, Choctaw, Pima, Cherokee, Lakota, Cree, and Seminole, to name a few.

I take great pride in the fact that many of the men in my immediate family have served our country including my father, uncles, brothers, sons, nephews, and cousins. It is believed that the reason Native Americans enlisted in groves is due to their strong tradition of warriors as leaders. It is ironic that Indians were forbidden to speak their native tongue and punished harshly when doing so and yet, the Navajo Codetalkers are credited for their part in winning the war by using their language.

Melvin settled down upon his return and had four children with a beautiful Indian girl that he married. My sis and I still think of her today as our sister. They had three girls and one son who is the spitting image of his father. Luther married but never had any children. Neither one of them were very big in stature. Luther was maybe 5'10 and had an average build. Melvin was a little shorter, like our dad. They stood maybe about 5'8"tall. Both boys liked to draw, and they were pretty good at it, usually cartoon pictures of Beetle Bailey. I had a stack of their letters saved up and treasured them dearly. They were all I had from them and I would read them over and over. When I was booted out of the house, my parents didn't let me take much, not even the car I worked so hard to get. So I don't know what happened to the letters.

We were so proud of our brothers for serving our country. They hadn't lost their partying habits when they got home, though. They had matured but still liked to have a good time. It was wonderful to see them again. Unfortunately, they would not have many years left to walk this earth.

Statistics show that, generally speaking, Native Americans have a shorter life expectancy than non-Indians do. Poverty, sub-standard living conditions, diet, diabetes, suicide, tragic accidents, alcoholism, oppression, hopelessness, all contribute to this sad state of affairs.

At 55 years of age, I was considered to be an elder in our tribe. If "home is where the heart is," then, Watersmeet is my home, even though I physically reside in the eastern portion of the Upper Peninsula. I have found my way back to my roots. No matter how long I am away, where I've been, what I've done, or how many name changes I've gone through, I am accepted for who I am, and I feel loved there.

BOYS, BOYS, BOYS

Like I said, all my friends and I talked about, were boys. With hormones flaring wildly, we were on a mission to see who would have bragging rights to the best looking boyfriend.

Native students had a female guidance counselor/tutor in school. At that time, programs were developed to address the high drop out rate of Native students. She somehow knew which girls had bad home lives and felt sorry for us. We were probably identified, because of our failing grades or misbehavior in school. Even though I enjoyed school, I was distracted by what was going on at home. Some of my grades were starting to suffer. She invited three of us to spend a week downstate where she was going home to visit. I don't know how she got my parents' permission, but I got to go with two other girls who were friends of mine.

It was probably about a 9 or 10-hour drive downstate to Grand Rapids. This was a city compared to our little hick town. She let us venture off on our own a little bit. We headed out to check out the area and found a nearby park. It wasn't long before a group of boys around our age came to check us out. We sat around puffing on our cigarettes and they pulled out their weed. They passed it around, and soon we were laughing, having a good 'ol time. We were all sitting in a circle on the ground, Indian-style. My friend D. and I noticed the boy sitting across from us. It was summer, everyone was wearing shorts, but this guy was going commando. We could tell because his shorts were really baggy and when he sat down you could see his whole package up his pant leg. He either didn't know or didn't care. We must have seen it at the same time because we both burst out laughing. They asked us what was so funny. We told them it must be the weed.

The place we were staying had a swimming pool in the back. The yard was fenced off from the neighbors. We had it all to ourselves. It was a warm night and dark enough to take our clothes off and go skinny-dipping. The water felt good, silky against our skin, and was our first skinny-dipping experience. The stars were out and shined brightly up above. For a little while it was as if we didn't have a care in the world. I didn't want to go back home.

But we did have to go back home and into the tenth grade. That year, three of my friends had gotten pregnant. Two of them dropped out of school. One of my friends found out she was pregnant, but stayed in school as long as she could. There was one mean girl, M., whom most were afraid of. You didn't want to cross her or you would get your ass kicked. I was very loyal to my friends and stuck up for them or anyone who got picked on, if I could. This girl's boyfriend was flirting with my friend. Actually he was a big flirt with a lot of girls, even me. Well, M. had heard he was chasing after someone and thought it was my friend, who was now pregnant. She told her she was going to kick her ass the first chance she got. I told her, "You'd better not touch her or I'll kick your ass." I thought I probably couldn't, but I sure couldn't let her hurt my friend and the baby inside. During the school day, M. left a note in my locker that said, "You fucking bitch I'm going to kill you after school." That had me shaking in my boots, but I knew I was going to have to face her, I had already ran my mouth. Word got around and a small group started forming outside waiting for the big fight they knew was going to be a good one.

I put my hair up in a ponytail and we stood facing each other. Kids were standing all around us yelling "get her, get her" to both of us. I wasn't one to just go up and start swinging unless I was really mad. She wasted no time grabbing me by my ponytail, and it was on. She tried to punch me in the face, but I put my head down and swung my fist as hard as I could and connected right in her mouth. She stumbled back, and when I looked up, her mouth was bleeding and her lip began to swell. We grabbed each other at the same time trying to throw each other down. When we hit the ground I landed on top of her and she wrapped her legs around my neck. She tried to kick me off but I had her pinned. By then a teacher came out and broke us up. After that happened, even though it was somewhat of a stalemate, she was nice to me.

That's how you have to stand up to a bully, otherwise, they just keep picking on you.

My friends and I talked often about sex. One of them had gotten her hands on some Playgirl magazines. We wanted to check out what men looked like naked. We giggled with curiosity and naivete and were surprised to learn that not everyone had black pubic hair. Hell, we didn't even know what was all up in our own deep, dark void. Biology wasn't our strongest class. We only knew there were many parts in the female anatomy, but did not know the exact location of them.

I had crushes but nothing that ever amounted to anything up until then. I had two serious boyfriends in high school. One was when I was a junior and the other in my senior year. My junior year, my boyfriend's name was T. His family had money and they were non-Indian. I had a thing for guys with blond hair for some reason. T. wasn't really even my type. Girls wanted guys with a nice body, big chest and arms, trim, strong legs, and a nice looking face. Isn't that what guys like too, a big chest and a nice butt? He pursued me every chance he got and that sent me the message that he really wanted me. He wasn't all that. He was even on the heavy side. He paid a lot of attention to me, was persistent and charmed me with his flattery. He had bought me a pretty necklace and earring set and some expensive perfume. I had to hide the jewelry and not let my dad know I got it from him or he probably would have made me give it back. I gave in and started wearing his class ring. I was a push-over then. It was hard for me to say no to a lot of things. I didn't want anyone to be mad at me or hurt. He had nice cars, and it was fun when he would let me drive them.

My adopted dad, after much begging, finally let me start dating T. He could pick me up at 7:00 p.m., but I had to be home by 11:00 p.m. He mostly just wanted to go parking. That didn't last too long because I was sitting on the hill one day with friends and saw him go driving by with another girl. She was too big or I would have kicked her ass. I gave him his ring back the next day. One of my friends told me he had asked her out too. He tried to get back with me, but I didn't want anything to do with him. He became kind of mean and ignorant to me after that. My dad told me it wouldn't have gone anywhere, anyway, because his family wouldn't have let him get serious with an Indian girl. By this time, my parents knew some girls my age were getting pregnant. I was old enough to have boyfriends, and they knew I would probably be sexually active. At my next doctor's visit they put me on a birth control pill.

I was desperate to prove, mostly to myself, that I could have a normal relationship. I needed to know that I could attract the opposite sex, not just my sick, perverted dad. Eventually, I thought it would lead to marriage with someone who could save me from my father. I was looking for my knight in shining armor. I wanted to have the family that I never had.

Usually the boys I was interested in were on the wild side, bad boys, and they wanted me to meet them at parties. The nice boys seemed boring. Maybe I thought it would have to be a "bad boy," that would stand up to my father and protect me. It was hard enough getting out of the house and the few times we got to hook up with boys, I always seemed to get caught. Our parents seemed to have their spies all over town watching for us. Sure enough, an aunt or uncle would see us riding around with some boys and call our parents. We were always getting grounded. Because I could hardly ever get out of the house, they usually hooked up with someone else. It hurt being betrayed but I knew there were more fish in the sea.

The only places we were allowed were basketball and football games, a few dances, or maybe sleepover at a friend's house now and then. Of course, we would go, stay for a little while at the games, just to say we were there, and then sneak out to chase boys. Most of them had cars, booze, and weed. We would have to find out the score of the game from someone and rush home before our parents got home from the bar and bingo. They always asked, "Who won and what was the score?"

One summer I attended a dance in town. Some boys we knew had gotten hold of some liquor. We went out back and choked it down. I got pretty drunk then realized I had to get home by my curfew or my parents would "call the cops." I could hardly stand up and knew I would be busted. I thought, "Fuck it, I'm not going home." I thought that I was going to be in trouble, grounded as usual anyway, and I would be grilled about who bought the liquor. I didn't want to get anyone in trouble.

I had a friend in L'Anse, and she was the only one I could think of that might help me out of my situation. I didn't want to hitchhike because I figured they would be driving around looking for me. So, I started the 4-mile walk around midnight. Every time I saw headlights, I jumped in the ditch and ducked down. It must have taken about 4 hours to get to L'Anse. I got there about 5:30 in the morning and hadn't slept all night. By the time I got there I was dirty and full of mud from jumping in the ditches. My friend answered her door and I told her that I had run away from home. We talked for a couple of hours and she persuaded me to go home. She knew someone who could give me a ride home.

When I got there, sure enough, the cops had been called. Surprisingly, my parents were more worried than angry with me. The cops put me in the back of the squad car and had a long talk with me about why I didn't come home. Here was my opportunity to get it all out. Then I remembered how the priest reacted when we tried to tell what was going on. I told them I was tired of our parents being so strict, that I had experimented with some booze, and was just too scared to come home. Our parents eased up a little after that.

The summer that I was turning a senior in school, an Indian family from North Dakota moved to town. They had two boys and a girl. One boy was my age and the other was my sister's age. They were so hot! F. had thick, black, wavy hair. He obviously worked out and had a lot of muscles. You could see the muscles in his legs bulging out right through his tight jeans. All the girls were instantly attracted when we saw him around while working our summer jobs. Their dad was the criminal investigator for the Bureau of Indian Affairs on the reservation. He stood about 6'4", very fit, and walked with an air of confidence. F. wasn't that tall, maybe 5'10", shorter like his mother. She was only around 5'0". He acted shy, easily smiled, but usually had his head down.

My friends and I couldn't stop staring and wondered who would capture his attention. He scoped out the girls, and when our eyes met, we smiled at each other. We eventually started talking to each other and the next thing you know, we were going steady. I gave him my senior ring that he wore on his pinkie. I never had trouble getting a boyfriend. The problem was keeping them. That never-getting-out–of-the-house situation seemed to doom me every time.

We went together for most of the school year. Sis went out with his brother for a while. He was good-looking like his brother. They made a cute couple. She had blossomed into quite the beauty. Sis had the most stunning blue eyes, and she had many boys pursuing her. She was a little more rough-and-tumble than I was. She was built a little bigger boned than I was. If my pants shrunk in the dryer, I would have her put them on and do some deep knee-bends to stretch them out. "You're such a bitch," she would say. "Please? I'll let you wear that top you wanted." She usually did what I asked of her.

Towards the end of the school year, F's family invited me to go to North Dakota with them for a visit. Surprisingly, I was allowed to go, and I couldn't have been happier. Something terrible was about to happen that may have effected his decision to let me go. Maybe it was because F.'s dad was in law enforcement, and my dad didn't want him to start asking questions about why he was so strict and untrusting. Anyway, maybe his guilt got the best of him, because he let me go to North Dakota with my boyfriend, and I had a great time. I enjoyed seeing a different part of the country. North Dakota was very hot in the summer. The terrain was very flat, with hardly a tree in sight. F's dad said that some people from there, who went to Michigan, couldn't stand it. He said that all of the trees made them feel claustrophobic. I thought that was funny. Their relatives lived on the reservation in Turtle Mountain. We mostly hung out and I found them to be warm, welcoming people.

All my friends were drinking in high school. Because we could never get to any parties, sis and I drank with our dad out at the camp on some weekends. Then when we were back in school on Monday, everyone was talking about all the fun they had. Well, we had stories too of getting buzzed up. I 'm pretty sure we were becoming teenage alcoholics. Sometimes it was easier just to get to the point of passing out, and when he fondled us at least we wouldn't know what was happening. By then, our dad was taking my mother's sleeping pills, tranquilizers, and pain pills, and dropping them into the beers he gave us. It seemed like our mom and my aunt always had a medicine cabinet full of drugs. That's where he got the supply to drug us out at the camp.

My mother was often sick or in the hospital having some kind of major surgery. Back then you weren't in and out the same day. She would be in there for a week or more. That gave my dad time to sneak into our bedroom. By then after years of his perversion, we knew in the middle of the night when you seen the flashlight coming, and the dark figure appeared in the doorway you were in for it. Even today I do not like to sleep with my back towards the door. I have to be able to see who or what's coming through the doorway.

On another occasion when sis was allowed to stay over at one of her friends' house, I had to go spend a night out at the camp. He got sloshed as usual. I turned into bed early, not wanting to get drunk and started watching the doorway. Here he came, flashlight in hand, and started pulling the covers off me. "Leave me alone," I told him. We started wrestling, but he was too strong. He started to pin me down on the bed. I started crying, again, and just wanted to give up in frustration and desperation. Suddenly, I just got so pissed I decided to let him have it with all I had. I lifted both of my feet, with my strong legs, pushed him off. He stumbled backwards and fell down. On his way down, he somehow smacked his face on the nightstand and his mouth started bleeding. He got a fat lip and I thought, good, let's see how you explain that one to mom.

The next day when we got home, I came in sullen as ever, and she spotted his fat lip. "What happened to you," she asked. He told her he tripped on the rug and fell on the table. I smiled to myself wishing I could tell her what really happened, but at least it made him sweat a little. Having to fight him off was still not the worse thing he had done. That was about to come next.

FROM BAD TO UNBEARABLE

One weekend out at camp, dad had brought, God knows what kind of drugs to spike our beer with. We drank heavily and didn't take long to pass out or I should say, black out. The next morning he showed sis and me some pictures he had taken the night before with his polaroid camera. It was so shocking I hate to even talk about it. I shouldn't feel shame or guilt. I have to remember that I was a victim.

Some were of himself with his pants pulled down to his knees, but not showing his face, just his naked crotch area. He was posing sideways and frontal. The next ones were of me. He had taken all of my clothes off and I was lying on the bed with my legs spread. He had raped me with some sort of instrument and then took pictures of it. We couldn't believe what we were looking at and gasped in horror. We couldn't believe what he had done. "Why would you do something like that, how could you," we asked. He threw them in the woodstove and didn't say anything. If he hadn't shown us, we probably wouldn't have known at all. "You're one sick fuck," I told him. He may as well have just urinated on me. He couldn't have humiliated me more.

I couldn't stand the sight of him and wanted to do something about it. Sis and I had often talked about how we wished he were dead. Now, with a more serious tone, when he couldn't hear us, we started talking about ways we could kill him. We knew he always drank himself into a stupor. It would be easy to wait until he passed out and have our way with him. We could maybe stab him to death, or take the axe and dismember him. He had a gun at the camp, we thought maybe we could shoot him as he slept. No, that would be too hard to explain to the cops. We thought a better idea would be to start the camp on fire. We could get out before the fire department got there. It would be too late for him. They might believe the woodstove somehow got out of control. He doesn't know how close he came to being burned alive. We spent more time talking ourselves out of it. The way we always got caught when we were up to no good, with our luck, we would be the ones going to prison. I was a terrible liar too. All of our catholic upbringing would cause me to 'fess up and take my licking. My conscience wouldn't allow me to do something like that.

Graduation was coming up soon. I had until fall before I turned 18. I knew I couldn't get out from under them until I became of legal age. The night of our graduation party, things were just getting hopping, and I only had about a half an hour before I had to be home by 11:00 p.m., or they would be calling the cops on me. That was always the threat. I was having a good time until this younger girl came staggering up to F. I was standing off to the side, and she was so drunk she didn't see me. She went to put her arms around his neck, and I started to walk over to her. She saw me and dropped her arms and walked away. "What was that all about?" I asked him. "I don't know," he said. I thought to myself, "Ya right."

Soon after that one of my friends told me he had gone out with her. I was mad as hell, and I knew I was going to pound her, first chance I got. The next weekend, I saw her walking down the street. I went up to her and told her that I knew she went out with my boyfriend. I threw her down in the mud and started wiping the mud all over her face. I didn't know her mother was a ways behind her. She came up to me, hollering, saying, "How would you like me to do that to you?" I told her, " that's what she gets for going out with my boyfriend." I wanted to break up with him then, but he talked me out of it. I thought I would give him another chance.

That summer I caught him cheating with one more girl who was younger and very pretty. Someone told me they saw him at a party with her. I spotted her downtown sitting on the hill with a few of her friends. Sis and I were driving by, and I pulled over. "Come on, I'm going to kick her ass, you keep her friends off me." I ran up that hill, jumped on her and started bitch-slapping her. One of her friends went to get up. Sis balled up her fist, stepped towards her and told her, "Sit the fuck down!" We left after that. Sis said, "Oh sure, you get one and I had to take on three?" I laughed and said, "Where'd you learn to talk so vicious, anyway?" "From you," she told me.

I had one more stop to make that day. I went straight to F's house and told him I wanted my ring back. He acted all tore up about it, but I didn't care. I wasn't hearing any more of his lies. We were done. The girl's boyfriend was in my graduating class. He and I had gotten Best Figure and Physique for class favorites. He was as good-looking as F. She went out with my boyfriend, so I made it a point to go out with hers. He had been asking me out for a while, anyway.

Once I graduated, I was still partying, but would make it home before my curfew. One night though, after a few beers, I came home to a dark house. It was only 10:30 p.m., I found that strange. Sis was in bed, Francis was in her room, and mom and dad were in their bedroom. I sat on the couch, for a few minutes, wondering what was going on. All of a sudden my mother came charging out, all 230 pounds of her. She went off on me and started slapping me, yelling what a whore I was and how sick of me she was. Then she said, "You might think I don't know what's going on around here, but I do!" That was a shocker. I thought, then why didn't you do something? She kept wailing on me, for some reason I called for my dad, to get her off me. "He isn't going to help you," she said. By then sis came out and didn't know if she should jump in and help me, or what to do. I finally lifted both of my feet and pushed her in her big stomach and shoved as hard as I could. It was just like what I had done to my dad that one night. She stumbled backwards a little and yelled to my dad that I was trying to kick her.

"Fine, I'll get out of here," I told her, crying. I ran for the door with her on my heels, tried to make it through the door, but she was trying to pull me back in by my shirt. I was holding on to the doorframe. Finally, she gave me a shove out the door that almost sent me sprawling to the ground. "Go on then, get the hell out of here, and don't you ever come back!" They even forbid me to see my sister. We would be separated once again.

Once I was outside I ran down the road a little ways then stopped. I thought to myself, "Now what do I do? Where can I go?" The only place I could think was my ex-boyfriend's house. I went there and told them what had happened. They said I could stay until I got a place of my own. I had been working up at the local tribal center. I managed to save up some money, enough to get an apartment. My parents wouldn't let me have any of my things at first. I finally got some of my clothes. I had a 10-speed bike I would ride to work; sometimes I hitchhiked the couple of miles. I knew someone would pick me up on the way to work. My parents wouldn't even let me take my car that I had worked so hard to get. They gave it to sis. When she left, a couple of years after I did, they didn't let her have it neither.

Two of my friends that I graduated with moved in with me to help out with rent. We started to party every night. I gained ten pounds that summer just from drinking. None of us knew how to cook. I was eating a lot of toast. Once I bought a roll of salami. I threw it in a pot of water and called my friend to ask her how long should I boil it before it was done. She laughed and said, "You don't boil salami!" Then I knew why it wasn't getting tender.

One warm night, we were hanging out, and a couple of my friends stopped by to have a few beers and get high. One of them was the same girl I was on the trip to Grand Rapids with a couple of years before. She and another friend stepped outside the apartment building only to come running back in a few minutes later laughing really hard. It was a one-floor level building and all of the apartments were one-bedroom and connected to each other. Someone a few doors down had their lights on, with see-through curtains. The girls saw some guy, sitting in a chair, getting a blow-job from a girl who was on her knees. The window was low enough, next to the sidewalk, to see everything inside. "Oh, my God, you have to see this," they giggled. We all walked by, checking it out, and then busted out laughing. They heard us out there and finally turned out their lights. It was funny that my friend and I spotted something obscene again at the same time.

I was quite buzzed up one night that summer and was going to walk downtown. It was dark in the neighborhood by our apartment. One guy I graduated with had been partying with us. He had asked me out during our schooldays, but he was not my type. I didn't know he was following me. He caught up to me and grabbed onto my arm. "Hey, wait up! I've always wanted to go out with you," he said. I told him I didn't want to go out with him. He started wrestling me down to the ground and was trying to pull off my clothes. He was too heavy to get off me. I was so scared I started crying and yelling for help. Dogs started barking, porch lights were going on, and he finally got off me. "Fine then, you bitch!" he said to me as he walked away.

It was that same summer that I found out what my "friends" thought of me. I was hanging out with a couple of my so-called friends for a while then decided to leave. As I walked away, I heard them start talking about me. They thought I was far enough away that I didn't hear or, maybe they hoped I would. They continued to discuss all of the partying I was doing. One guy was the same one who begged me to go out with him and had just broken up with his girlfriend for going out with my ex. He told them that a few beers and anyone could have anything from me. They all started laughing. I just kept walking like I hadn't heard them.

I walked down to the dock by the lake. I felt an overwhelming sadness come over me. There I sat, for I don't know how long, with my legs swinging back and forth over the water, staring at the bottom, and contemplating killing myself. All I had to do was fall into the water. I couldn't swim, and I knew it was over my head. Maybe then all of the pain would finally stop. I had nothing to live for. I was thinking about how my real parents had left me. My adopted parents threw me out of the house, I didn't have a boyfriend, no friends to speak of, I couldn't see my sister, and my brothers were gone into the service. Everyone I knew and trusted had taken advantage of me in some way. Even God had abandoned me, I thought. I couldn't think of one person here on this earth that would even miss me if I were gone. That truth really hurt. No one wanted me. No one cared, or loved me. Why was I even born? Why was I being punished? I was so tired of life shitting on me. At that moment I didn't want to go on living. I didn't have the strength to go on another day. I thought to myself, just do it, do it. I was crying, sobbing, and my heart ached so bad, like so many times before. I just couldn't take it any more.

I couldn't do it. Something, some little bit of self-preservation I had left inside made me question what I was doing. I told myself to get up and leave right now before I changed my mind. I started walking slowly back towards town. Just then one of my cousins spotted me and asked if I wanted to get high. "Of course," I told him. I knew I could forget about what had just happened, if only for a while. "Suck it up," I said to myself. "I'll give it a little longer, see what happens." I knew partying would dull the pain. I guess I realized I was out of that house, the abuse had finally stopped, but now I was doing it to myself. I was one hot mess!

FINALLY A FAMILY

I continued to drown my sorrows by drinking. The drinking age back in 1976 was 18. True, I had a couple of months to go, but sometimes minors who looked old enough could get served. I was in the bar shooting some pool when in walked another blond-haired, good-looking guy, slim and fit. " Mmmm, who do we have here," I wondered to myself. I had never seen him before. He watched me as I shot then finally came up to me and said something about me needing a lesson on how to shoot. He showed me how to bank a shot. There was some kind of attraction between us. He was older, I could tell, but that didn't stop him from flirting with me. Come to find out he had moved into the apartment complex next to me; actually his brother owned the apartment buildings. I had seen him outside the apartments and was hoping to get to know him better. He reminded me of John Denver with his straight, somewhat long, blond hair, and wire-rimmed glasses. There was something arrogant about him, though. He seemed a little too sure of himself. I had enough confidence, too, that when I wanted someone I would somehow get him, but he acted as though he could take me or leave me.

He played hard to get, dating a few other people, before asking me out. He knew I was close to legal age. He had just gotten out of the service and moved up from downstate. He came from a large Polish, Catholic family. There were eight boys and five girls in his family. Most of his brothers had moved up to Baraga and were in the construction business. The men in his family were all very handsome and had beautiful wives. We saw them in church often. He seemed worldly to me, coming out of the army and having lived in a city. He seemed to be an authority on everything, or, at least, thought he was. I hadn't really been out of the Upper Peninsula, except for that trip to North Dakota.

I was just a country bumpkin.

We finally started dating, when I turned 18, and he then wanted me to go off the pill. I told him I would probably end up getting pregnant, and he said he didn't care. Finally, someone wanted to have a future with me. We partied like rock stars, he showed me a good time, and we enjoyed being with each other.

He was the first man to ever take me to a motel and spend the night together. In the morning, he took me out for breakfast. I never really ate out at restaurants either. I ordered bacon, eggs, and toast. When the waitress asked how I wanted my eggs, I didn't know what you called it, I only knew I didn't like the yolk soft. That grossed me out. So I shrugged my shoulders and just said, "Ah, cooked." They both laughed at me. I wonder what their reaction would have been if I would have said "fertilized."

He was kind of an out-doorsy person. That appealed to me because I loved being out in the woods. He liked to hunt and fish. They had a family camp with a sauna where we would spend some weekends. We did some target shooting at cans. I think it surprised him that I could handle a gun.

Our dad taught us how to shoot a gun, and I was a pretty good shot. I absolutely loved being outside, doing any activity, the more physical the better. I didn't particularly like being on the water, though. When I went swimming, I wouldn't go in water over my head. Boats made me nervous. I didn't like fishing either. I didn't like touching worms and I thought the fish could bite me. One time when I was asked to pick up a dozen nightcrawlers, I asked the clerk if there was any way that they could get out of that container. He just gave me a puzzled look. I put them on the floor in the back seat of my car. I could just picture all 12 of them pushing the cover up and off with their heads then crawling onto my seat and getting all over me. I would have freaked out and probably wrecked my car.

I got pregnant about six months later and we got married shortly thereafter. My sister was my maid of honor, of course. My father gave me away and cried like a baby while he walked me up the aisle. I didn't know if it was over the guilt of what he had done or having to accept the fact that I no longer belonged to him. We married in a log church over-looking Lake Superior. His oldest brother's construction company built the beautiful pine log church. The priest was at one time one of the people who use to drive kids to Harbor Springs. He was now a close friend of my husband's family.

When my first-born arrived, I had to deliver him by C-section, due to complications. I was nursing him for a couple of months when I got pregnant with my second son. So, in 1978, I had two children, one born in January and the other in December. My dream was coming true of having a real family. We both wanted kids but I was only able to have four due to the c-sections. I always had wanted a girl that looked like me. She finally came after two boys. My youngest son came two years later. I felt so blessed and happy. The long-awaited family I never had was finally complete. They all had their father's lighter hair but my brown eyes. I couldn't believe how beautiful and precious they were, and still are. We attended mass weekly at the same church where we got married. Our children were all baptized there also.

I volunteered to help clean the church, taught catechism, and later played the organ. The few years of lessons were finally put to good use. At times the congregation giggled when I played the wrong notes. The organ had a pedal, similar to one in a car, and you had to push it down for the volume to get louder. I wasn't quite sure how far down it needed to be when I began a song. Once, I had it too far and everyone jumped on the first note. I always did have a lead foot.

Not long after I had gotten married, our father had a stroke. I figured God had finally punished him for what he had done to us. He didn't have much use in one of his legs, but he could still get around. He continued to drink. I hardly ever took my kids around him. He didn't deserve to see the grandchildren, and I wouldn't have trusted him to be around them anyway.

That same year, I had gotten a phone call from my adopted mother. She said that my sister had gotten into some trouble with a boy. She got caught with him in her bedroom. The cops were called, and she had told them that our father had been sexually abusing us for years. She wanted to know if it was true. I told her "yes." She asked why we hadn't told her. I told her that I thought she knew.

Our dad was threatening to kill himself, but didn't. No charges were ever pressed. Not long after that she dropped out of high school, with only one semester to go, and then moved out west with her boyfriend. Incest was an issue not talked about back then and still isn't today. People tended to look the other way. Some of his relatives, of course, didn't believe us. What we thought would happen, did happen. They were saying, "After all they did for those girls! They have the nerve to say something like that!"

Sis wasn't gone for too long before she came back home. She had broken up with her boyfriend. She decided to move to Milwaukee with our real mother. They were able to make up for some of the lost years. I finally went to Milwaukee also for a visit. Some healing from the past had taken place and we were able to establish a relationship with our mother. We all had a good time together, going out to eat, and shopping at the malls. "Sure is a big town," I told them. "City, Linda, it's called a city," they responded.

This would be my first experience with an escalator. Mom and sis stepped on and up they went. I couldn't do it. Every time I went to step on, I would pull back, because another step would appear. I thought my foot would somehow get caught in there and I kept hesitating. Sis came back down around and tried to show me again. "Just step on," she said and up she went again. I was moving the top half of my body but my feet didn't want to go. By then a small crowd was starting to form behind me waiting to get on. I finally conquered that. Then we came to a revolving door. I had never been in one of those either. The compartment looked big enough to fit two people so I stepped in after my mom. She turned around and was surprised to see me right in her face, taking baby steps on her heels so I wouldn't get hit in the ass with the next door. They found it all quite amusing.

Our mother told us stories of when she was with my dad in Watersmeet. She said after she left us, she use to go back for visits. She even stayed with my dad briefly. Our real dad and my brother Melvin had gotten into a bad car accident and were nearly killed. They both suffered broken bones and were in the hospital for quite a while. One of my half-sisters had came from Kansas to take care of them. She must have been about 12 or 13 years old. She stayed until she completed school. I thought back to what had happened to me under the covers after my mother left. I figured she was probably enduring the same kind of abuse I was at the same time, only by our biological father. Either way, no matter who raised me, fate had determined that I would suffer sexual abuse.

Cracks were starting to appear in our marriage during this time. There were a number of reasons why this happened. My first husband's childhood years had left him scarred. Having 13 children would have been overwhelming for anyone. Parents sometimes take their frustrations out on their kids. The stories of abuse that he and his siblings described were pretty awful. They received beatings from their parents that no child should have to endure. I can understand why the bonds formed amongst them were very strong. Maybe this is the reason why he spent so much time with his brothers rather than with our kids and me. Their daily routine was to sit at the coffee shop for hours on end, philosophizing and solving the world's problems. They were of the "old school" mentality that believed a woman's place is in the home and she should be seen but not heard, or so it seemed. That made me feel more like a child than a wife.

Therefore, being the man of the house, he made all of the major decisions, and confided in his brothers rather than me. He was slightly older, more experienced, and it seemed that he couldn't depend on me to be his equal. I felt that what I said didn't matter and was of no importance. I was beginning to feel inferior, insignificant, and lonely. It is a different kind of loneliness when the one you love is physically present but emotionally absent. I think their father didn't do much with his sons either. He was probably too busy working trying to support all of those kids. My ex never got the attention therefore he didn't know how to give it to our kids. He was able to hug them, kiss them, and tell them that he loved them, as he did with me, but we needed more.

We got married at a young age also. It seemed as though it was what we wanted at the time. Sometimes as you grow and change, it is only then, that you know what you really want and need out of life. Maybe we got married for the wrong reasons. We were two needy people with baggage that would later trip us up. My neediness may have been just too much for him.

We partied excessively, which didn't help our marriage. We both did drunken, stupid, obnoxious things to each other. Like most men, he had a wandering eye for pretty women. I felt as though the desire in his eyes was for others, not me. My childhood trauma wouldn't allow me to let it roll off my shoulders. Another factor that affected my feelings was my hormonal imbalance during my pregnancies. The familiar feelings of insecurity, uselessness, and betrayal surfaced again.

He was young and healthy but did not have a steady job. He was very talented and skilled with his hands, when he chose to work. So, we had very little money to go around for food, necessities, or extras that the kids might have wanted. The interior of our house was unfinished and we had no running water. We had to haul water and shit in a bucket for a couple of years. I remember being 8 months pregnant and carrying a 5-gallon bucket of water in each hand into the house. I don't know how he did it, when emptying that bucket when it was full, but he never spilled a drop. Our life was hard with 4 little ones. Now they were the ones getting bathed in the same bath water, in a washtub, like I did when I was their age. We had to depend on our neighbor or his brother to get our water. I knew this was an annoying inconvenience for them.

I tried to stretch out the food to make it go as far as it could. I scraped their leftovers back into the pan for the next meal. I sometimes went without eating so they could have my share. One Christmas, we had a small tree, but there were no presents under it. It reminded me of growing up in Watersmeet.

We finally became "sick and tired" of being "sick and tired." It was at that point that we quit drinking together. We thought that would improve our circumstances. We were starting to get "our shit" together. There was still a distance between us though, for some reason.

I finally learned how to cook and would bake homemade bread and cookies. We lived on commodities from the tribe. Having four children, my car would be loaded to the roof with canned goods, cheese, flour, etc. Sometimes we found bugs in the food but at least it was something to eat. He was a neat-freak, but I didn't mind because I enjoyed cleaning house. I was just trying to please him in every way.

I always tried to take pride in my appearance. I walked 3 miles daily up the big hill out where we lived. I couldn't afford new clothes but I hit up plenty of rummage sales for the kids and myself. Every once in awhile I would forget to take the masking tape that read 25 cents off their shirt or pants and someone would see it and laugh.

Once the kids were in school full-time, I started to take college classes here and there. I also convinced him to let me go back to work. He and his brothers didn't like the wives interrupting their coffee clutching but I stopped by there a couple of times. Before I left, I was told not to do anything that was "going to get me fired," as again, the joke was on me. I thought he had a dry sense of humor and most of the time had to make myself laugh at his jokes, so he wouldn't feel bad. I could make them laugh at my Pollack jokes. One night I had finally run out and they asked, "don't you know any more Pollack jokes?" "You mean, other than you two?" I asked as I pointed at them. Even they had to laugh at that one.

We had a modest income from my job so I bought myself a few work clothes that were on sale, of course. I found a nice winter coat that was very pretty. It was a white, synthetic fur that looked as if it were real fox fur. It looked more expensive than it actually was. I was wearing it one day when I went to the tribal center to pick up my commodities. I walked into this one coming. There must have been about 20 people, or so, standing in line. I was toward the front of the line and one of my cousins was standing toward the back of the line. He spotted me up front and yelled out for everyone to hear, "Christ Linda, picking up your commods in your fur coat, got your limo parked out front too?!" Everyone started to laugh including me. Another funny joke that he use to like to tell goes, "Do you know why Indians can't take family portraits?" "No, why?" "Because when you tell them to say cheese, they all stand in a line." I resembled that remark just then.

My children's father didn't particularly like to be around my family. They were friendly enough to him but just coming from different cultures, I would guess, made him uncomfortable. I was equally uncomfortable around his family at times. I thought that if they knew my background that they would somehow judge me and think less of me. Our life pretty much revolved around his family. He didn't go to visit my relatives with me. He didn't want to go and help me get our commodities. He didn't come with me to the tribal clinic when the kids were sick. I thought people were probably wondering why my man wasn't accompanying me.

I was a low-maintenance kind of woman, I thought. I wanted what any woman wants from her husband. That is to be treated like he treated you when you first met. That is time alone together, attention, respect, gratitude, sincerity, etc. A ride in the woods, a walk down the road together, sitting by a campfire, talking earnestly about our dreams, fears, hopes, likes, and dislikes, these small things can go a long way. If he liked the way I smelled, cooked, looked, dressed, would it kill him to tell me so? I guess I just wasn't worth the effort. These were things that had stopped some time ago, along with the "I love you's". So, I quit saying it too. I just started doing my own thing. I joined a softball team, played volleyball, and visited my sister.

We had sobered up through the wonderful program of Alcoholics Anonymous (AA). It was a great brotherhood and we made many friends. We learned a lot about the disease of alcoholism. We were growing in some ways but becoming strangers in other ways.

Our standard of living had improved through the help of the tribe and the Bureau of Indian Affairs (BIA). The BIA funded a well and septic for us. The Keweenaw Bay Tribe allotted us a Home Improvement grant to finish the interior of the house. We had arrived to the twentieth century with running water and a toilet that flushed!

1980'S: THE LOST DECADE

I can't say the 1980's were all bad, but that was when I experienced the most devastating events of my life, even worse than the sexual abuse. The most exciting events were the birth of my daughter and my youngest son in 1980 and 1982. Their father and I finally sobered up in 1983. We had decided we had to become more responsible so our kids wouldn't see us for the drunks that we were.

Two years before we quit drinking, my brother Luther had returned home from the service. He had came out to visit me a few times. Melvin even showed up a couple of times. They finally met their niece and nephews. They were still partiers, so when we quit, their visits were somewhat awkward.

Luther had a way of getting under people's skin. My first husband did something for my brother that still stands out to me. We let Luther crash at our house one night. It was clear he hadn't bathed for a couple of days. He had taken his shoes and socks off before falling asleep on the couch and you could smell them from across the room. It was just before we got running water. We heated our water in a big pan on our woodstove. My ex took his stinky, filthy, dirty socks and hand washed them in the sink. He hung them by the woodstove to dry. Luther was glad to have clean socks to put on and thanked him the next day. I also told him that was a very thoughtful thing to do.

Memorial Day weekend, 1981, I got a phone call from my cousin's wife. She said she heard from someone in Watersmeet that Luther had shot himself, and that was all she knew. About an hour later, a tribal police officer pulled up in my driveway. He verified that Luther had died by committing suicide. He was very sorry to give me such bad news. I still couldn't believe it, so I called someone from Watersmeet and asked what happened. I couldn't imagine what could make him do something like that. Didn't he know how it would destroy us? They told me it was true, that he did not make it, he was dead. I started wailing and knew I had to track down sis to give her the horrible news.

I remember I couldn't sleep that night. I stayed up most of the night sobbing and crying. It felt as though I was still in shock. My ex told me to just quit crying because that wasn't going to bring him back. I thought he was one cold prick. I couldn't just "shut it off," because I needed to grieve my brother.

During the middle of the night, while everyone was sleeping, I walked downstairs to get a drink of water. We had a large window in the kitchen and you could look out into the woods at all of the trees. As I got myself a drink from the sink, my back was facing the window. You couldn't see into the darkness outside, only the reflection of the kitchen. As I stood there drinking my water, suddenly, I had a very strong sense that someone or something was directly outside the window staring in at me. It almost paralyzed me with fear. I have been told that when a loved one passes on, you should stay indoors, some say you should even cover all of your mirrors. This is because our loved one might be lost on his/her journey. They may be frightened and want someone from the family to go with them. I was so petrified that I could not bring myself to look out that window. I knew with every ounce of my being that if I did, I would see Luther. I ran back upstairs to bed. I have also been told that when a loved one dies that their spirit comes to visit their family.

Sis and I left for Watersmeet as soon as we could the next day. Mom, Dad, Melvin, cousins, aunts, uncles, and friends were all there. They had begun to prepare for the funeral. They told us what they knew had happened. They said that a bunch of them had been drinking at a baseball tournament. Luther got into a fight with one of our cousins, got his nose broke, then went home where he lived with my dad. He took a 30-30 rifle, laid on his bed, and shot himself in the head. My father had came home and found him. He said he thought Luther was sleeping at first. Dad grabbed the gun out of his hands and asked him, "What are you doing with that?" He then realized, as he looked closer, what he had done. I'm sure he didn't kill himself because of the fight. I think it may have been the straw that broke the camel's back. He probably had as much internal pain from our broken family, boarding school, and abuse, as we had.

To this day, I like to shoot handguns, shotguns, rifles, but I will not touch a 30-30. When the Veteran Honor Guard shot the 21-gun salute at the cemetary, I about jumped out of my skin. It reminded me of the fatal shot that Luther had done to himself and what it must have sounded like. My legs were shaking so hard when they played taps for my brother I thought I was going to collapse. Melvin took the news equally hard. He couldn't even attend the burial. They were as closely bonded as sis and me. I could see him standing way back watching from afar. "Melvin should be here," I told my dad. "Melvin is handling it the way he needs to," my dad told me.

We scraped up enough money to buy him a new shirt and pants to be buried in. The few clothes he had were quite worn and we wanted him to look nice. We didn't have enough money to buy new underwear for him and didn't want him to meet the Creator going commando. I remember our youngest sister stole a pair out of a package from the store and put them in her pocket. I felt guilty about that and had to confess our stealing to the priest during confession the next weekend.

My Aunt sewed him a pair of new moccasins for his journey and made him a tobacco pouch, filled with items that he would need as he walked on. Someone made him a beaded medallion also. It needed to be slipped over his head. It was an open-casket. Most of the damage from the self-inflicted wound was to the back of his head. We needed to lift his head. My mother looked at us and said, "I can't do it." "I can't either," I said. At that, my two sisters lifted his head and placed the medallion on him.

It was so hard to say goodbye to our brother. Our parents were very strong. I think they held it together for our sake. He had a great send-off; a traditional burial with all of our relatives and many friends in attendance. If he only knew how much he was loved, maybe he wouldn't have done what he did. I thought he must know now. He must be looking down at all of the people gathered and all of the tears being shed for him.

Just about every time I pulled into Watersmeet, I used to see Luther walking down the side of the road, on his way to the projects. After the funeral, when I came to town, I still looked for him on the side of the road, expecting to see him, then remembered that he was gone.

I felt it necessary to write a letter to Melvin after Luther died. I wrote him that maybe we hadn't told Luther enough how much we loved him. I wrote Melvin that I didn't want anything to ever happen to him without him knowing how much I loved him. I told him sis and I knew that we had missed out on so much without our brothers.

Three years later, I got a phone call from my cousin who told me Melvin had been in a car wreck. They didn't know anything else, but that it was bad. The next call that came was the news that Melvin had died from his injuries. It was too much. I couldn't believe it was happening again. It was surreal. Could it be true that we would never be able to see our brothers again?

They said he had been drinking and was racing with his friend. They were coming back from Land O' Lakes, WI, on the border, to Watersmeet. They had just re-paved the highway. It had been raining lightly and the roads were slick. They came to a curve in the road when Melvin lost control as he was passing his friend. They thought that maybe his tie rod broke. Another friend in the car with him, who sat on the passenger side, said that Melvin had the needle buried. His friend was thrown from the car as it flipped end over end, became air-born, and hit a tree. The steering wheel was the cause of Melvin's internal injuries. When I seen pictures of the car, it looked as though it had been through a car crusher at a junkyard, crinkled like an accordion.

I had to go find my sister again and tell her the bad news. We rushed to Watersmeet again to be with our family. I felt worse for our parents, who had to bury their only two sons. Both boys had traditional Indian burials. As they had at Luther's funeral, the sacred drum was played as they sang honor songs in Ojibway. Each beat, representing the heartbeat of Mother Earth, could be felt beating in unison with our own heartbeat. An elder from the tribe prayed in Ojibway to the Creator and the four directions. He spoke in our native tongue and then translated it to English. He had told them how to find their way on their journey to the spirit world.

When I returned home, I started to think about that letter I sent to Melvin. Why did I do that? Had I tempted fate and in some way brought it all on? I started to become obsessed with death. They say that when someone is reckless with their life, they too, are suicidal. I remembered that day when I sat at the end of the dock. I realized that life is so precious and sometimes taken for granted. I knew we should be grateful for every day the Creator gives us, for it is such a short time. We could be here one day, then gone the next, without having reached our full potential or finding true happiness.

I thought about our birth order, Luther was gone, now Melvin, and I was next in line. I really did not think I was going to live to see 30. Luther was only 25 when he passed and Melvin was only 27. I'll bet they had goals and dreams for their futures. We were just starting to get to a place where we had gotten our brothers back, only to lose them. We were building a relationship with them, getting to know each other, and making up for all of those years we didn't have together. It all felt so unfair. When they died, a part of us died with them. But, a part of them lives on, too, through us. I had to hold on to that.

I began to question very seriously, "Is this all there was to life? Would I ever find true happiness before I died? Would I be able to find and fulfill the purpose of my being? Was that purpose to be an example of how much pain a person could suffer? My heart was heavy and broken, I felt like I was headed for a major breakdown. I stayed sober, but I was so unhappy with my life. A sense of impending doom washed over me again.

It was around that time that I went to a trauma center in Wisconsin. It was a residential treatment place that specialized in sexual abuse issues. I knew that was at the root of my problems and I needed help to deal with my past. I knew I wanted out of my marriage. I couldn't take any more abuse, of the mental kind. If my husband didn't think I was all that he thought he wanted and needed, then let's just go our own separate ways. He could go find someone else to torture, play games, withhold his love, and do a "mind-fuck," with. I wanted to leave before I was left.

Besides having my four children, this treatment center experience was the most significant blessing for me. I finally had found some answers. With the help, support, and encouragement of professionals, I was able to go to those deep recesses in my mind that had always terrified me. I really thought that if I dared to go there I would not be able to find my way back. They helped me to realize that I was a survivor. I had not only survived the abuse, but I survived looking at the truth. What doesn't kill you really does make you stronger.

I thought I had it so bad, but there are always others out there that have it much worse. Listening to other victims' stories was equally difficult. I heard stories of victims that had been gang-raped, had lived a life of prostitution at a young age, and others that were sexually abused by family members, like myself.

The therapy was very intense. Psychiatrists, psychologists, group therapy, art therapy, all played a part in my treatment. They broke me down to the point that I was put on suicide watch, but then built me back up. The breaking point was when I was told to go back to the time that was most traumatic in my life and describe myself. When I verbalized what that little girl must have looked like, sickly, dirty, hungry, neglected, abandoned, and unloved. I almost couldn't take it. I felt so sorry for myself. I started to sob and could not stop. I cried through my whole hour-long session with my doctor and then went back to my room and kept crying the rest of the day. By evening, I had wept every tear out of my body. My eyes were so swollen from crying that I could hardly open them. Not once did the doctors hug me to comfort me. They told me that I needed to comfort that little girl inside myself. I had to give her what she needed.

They told me I didn't need a white knight in shining armor to save me, that, instead, I could save myself. I needed to tell myself that I was going to be okay. I had to love myself. I had to discover my own strengths, talents, goals and dreams. More importantly, I could attain what I wanted for myself. After all, God doesn't make junk. They reminded me of how much I had survived already and told me to recognize my own resiliency. I had to make decisions in my life. I did know that I didn't want to continue living in limbo and I didn't want to go on being treated like I had been.

I found the strength to call my husband and tell him that I wanted a divorce. He came down for a visit and was furious. He was taller than I, so he bent down, put his hands on his knees, and was now eye-level. He told me, with his condescending tone and about six inches from my face, "Without me you were nothing, you are nothing, and you'll never be nothing, is that what you want?" "I guess so," was all I could reply. If I had any doubt in my mind, that one sentence convinced me, it was what I wanted.

Going back home was not easy. I had to face the children and tell them what was happening. He had the support of his entire family but I had no one to lean on. I was told that if I wanted to break up the family then I would be the one moving out, not him, and he wasn't letting me have the children. He also said that I could leave with what I came to him with, nothing. How very clever, to use the one thing that meant anything to me, my children, in order to punish me.

I felt this was the only solution left for me. The adage, "If nothing changes, then, nothing changes" applied. We had tried marriage counseling in the past and it didn't help. I tried to communicate what my issues were and because he was getting everything he wanted, he couldn't see what the problem was.

Leaving my children was the most difficult thing I ever had to do. I knew it would be painful, but knowing what I had been through, I knew they would be alright. I wasn't going to walk out of their lives never to be heard from again, like what had been done to me.

During the divorce, I had signed the house over to my ex, since I was told to leave and couldn't take my children. They would need a roof over their head. I didn't want or ask for anything, except for my clothes. At first, he considered burning them, but then gave them to me. Some people become vindictive and vengeful when a divorce occurs and I was starting to feel the wrath of his anger. I thought I was giving him what he really wanted deep down.

I had completed my Associates degree and was determined to achieve my Bachelor's degree next, as quickly as I could. My plan was to get my degree, so I could make a better life, then get physical custody of my kids. Things did not go as I had hoped. The ex finally stepped up and became a great dad and continues to be to this day. He then went on to college and got a job in Corrections. Why he couldn't do that when we were married, I do not know. In some ways, it seemed as though it took my leaving for him to take an interest in the kids, get a job, and get more out of life.

At that time, plans for a new maximum-security prison was being discussed in Baraga. This would be bringing many new, good paying jobs to the area. A public meeting was held to allow residents to express their opinions. The tribe was an integral part of the community that contributed in many ways. Someone in the crowd wanted to know where the tribe stood on the issue. One of my friends, who attended, told me that someone yelled out, "fuck the Indians!" She said tribal members were astounded and looked to see who the idiot was. They were surprised to see that it was my ex-husband. I tried to teach my children to be proud of their Indian heritage but that attitude, coming from their father, probably made them feel shameful for being part Indian.

I feel he, and some of his family, and others in town who enjoy kicking people when they are down, only spread the worse about me, blamed me, ostracized me, and called me every name in the book. It felt like I was being run out of my own hometown. His family had moved up from the Lansing area. I only knew that they could not possibly do or say anything that could cause more pain than what I had already been through in my lifetime. So, they could just go ahead and take their best shot, or better yet, go fuck themselves. I had taken enough shit from everybody.

By now the 1980's were almost over. Where those years went, I really don't know. It was pretty much a blur. I can't say there was no one there for me. It seemed like it but that's because I thought I had to go through my mess alone. My sister and cousins, and a few friends that I hadn't lost in the divorce, continued to be there for me. When I did run into them their kind words and encouragement got me through the sadness.

Music always played a part in lifting my spirits too. I like pop, and old rock, but my favorite is country music. Maybe because that's what we constantly heard being played by Aunt Francis. I knew all of the popular singers like Eddie Arnold, Buck Owens, Johnny Horton, Waylon Jennings, Tammy Wynette, Loretta Lynn, George Jones, to name a few. I've been known to belt out a song in the shower or while bustling around the kitchen. I like to crank it up, singing and dancing around while doing housework. It seems to motivate me. I also pass the time singing out of tune to the radio while driving down the road.

I cannot say I know the contemporary pop songs or artists from the 1980's though. There was so much pain going on during that decade that I don't know who or what was popular. I lost a big part of my life when those that I loved the most had been taken from me.

Organized religion had also played a major role in my life. Getting divorced in the Catholic Church meant that I could no longer receive the sacrament of communion. It was then that I started to consider myself a "fallen-away Catholic." After all of the hypocrisy I had witnessed from the priests, nuns, and others who claimed to be good people, I wanted to seek out the spiritual way of life that my ancestors practiced. I had a lot of gratitude and tried to remember to thank the Creator every day for everything I did have. I have a lot of love for my children, grandchildren, relatives, and close friends. I try to show them just what they mean to me.

I am still an advocate for the underdog. My heart goes out to the underprivileged, and the down trodden. I refuse to keep being a victim and avoid people who want to treat me badly through their negativity, jealousy, sarcasm, criticism, or other actions. It's better to stay away because my violent tendencies from the past want to resurface. After all, I come from a long line of "cray-cray."

MOVING ON

While going through the divorce, I moved to Marquette, MI, to transfer my credits and complete my Bachelor's degree at Northern Michigan University (NMU). I worked part-time at the college and took classes full-time. I had hurt my ex and it seemed to be his mission to make my circumstances so difficult that I would come crawling back to him. He threatened to sue the treatment facility for "talking me into the divorce." My mother was confronted by him and blamed for me being "so screwed up in the head." I tried to obtain a small loan from the bank to help me get on my feet and intended to repay the note with my financial package from NMU. The banker told me that my ex told him not to give me a dime. I reminded him that it was my name on the payroll checks that was making the house payments. I was able to secure the loan and repaid it in a short time.

What was supposed to be "happily ever after" turned sour, and there seemed to be no fixing it. He had gotten everything so I didn't understand why he couldn't move on. His true self was revealed to me through his actions. It was difficult to focus on school when I was constantly trying to defend myself. I had to go to court to address his complaints. If the kids came home sick from their visits with me, it was because my house was dirty. He didn't like the fact that I did not take them to church, he wouldn't give me my daughter because he didn't want to split up the kids, and then he had them each write me a letter. They were too young to know what a bitch, whore, and slut meant. They also wrote that I was no longer their mother. One weekend, while back in town, my tire had gotten slashed. I could have stooped to this low level but didn't. I had friends at school and being in counseling, is what got me through it. A couple of my friends had been through a divorce and shared similar stories about bitter ex-husbands. They insisted that it would get better. They said that one day my children would be old enough to understand all that had happened.

As part of my follow-up treatment, they had recommended a therapist in Marquette that had expertise in the area of sexual abuse. It is hard to find a doctor that specializes in this issue. She used a resource book titled, "Courage to Heal," by Ellen Bass & Laura Davis. I've read that the book had faced criticism but it helped others and me in our group. It gave me insight into why I had relationship issues. We explored the damaged areas that I faced in my life such as abandonment, trust, and low self-esteem. We also discussed the unhealthy coping skills I had developed.

One exercise that was suggested was to write a letter to my abuser, my adopted dad who was still alive, and let him know how the sexual abuse affected my life. I did this and poured out my heart in the 2-page letter. I wrote of the pain, disgust, and shame. He called me a few days later and told me that he was sorry. Somehow, it did not give me the healing that I thought would come with the reveal. At least he knew that I knew, it wasn't a dream, it really happened, it wasn't my fault, it was all on him.

I was trying to get on with life and deal with the post traumatic stress disorder simultaneously. My weaknesses caused two more failed marriages down the road. At the same time I was able to somehow graduate and take on new challenges.

I attempted to do an introspection, which is an honest look into self, and work on changing those self-defeating shortcomings. I found it to be an up-hill battle. My problems were complicated and multi-faceted. My "normal" was not normal. As I psychoanalyze myself, I can recognize my patterns. I have the awareness. I get swept up by all of the attention and promises. It feels like I have found what I need. Maybe these men are just as needy as I am, and I choose that type so I can save them. I need to feel useful to prove to myself that the message I was sent for most of my life was wrong. I do have something to offer. Maybe that's my destiny, men get what they want from me, then I dust them off, build them up, and send them on their way to find someone better than me. I forget to take care of myself. I see what I do, but keep repeating the same mistakes thinking next time will be different. I have lots of love to give and want to work equally with my partner towards a comfortable life.

My second marriage came about more as a rebound from an unhappy marriage. Not wanting to be alone, I thought that if a good prospect came along, I would give it another try. I was in college and was out with a girlfriend at a comedy club. Sitting next to us was a very attractive guy who introduced himself to me. He was from Florida and was working in Marquette temporarily, as a field specialist in telecommunications. He was a little younger than me, another blond-haired beauty with a sweet southern accent, and was quite the charmer. He told me he was previously married also, but for a short time. I think he was rebounding from a "marriage gone bad," also.

Actually, he made my head spin with all of the attention, flattery, and gifts he showered on me after we started dating. He treated me like a lady, opening doors, pulling my chair out, very thoughtful and considerate, quite the gentleman. It was just the opposite treatment from what I had the previous 12 years. He was very generous and gave me experiences I never had. I felt like putty in his hands. He made me think and feel like he would do anything for me. I felt as though I had been swept right off my feet.

After being treated like I was nothing, now someone was treating me as if I was a queen. I mean, limousines, jewelry, nice clothes, and trips to Florida, expensive dinners at fine restaurants, and staying in the best hotels. We had long talks about anything and everything. He enjoyed being in my company and we had a lot of fun together. He even flew my kids to Florida for a vacation. It was a new experience for them too–flying and visiting Florida. I never asked for anything for my kids from him. Having no children of his own, he enjoyed spoiling my kids and spending time with them.

So, it was a whirlwind romance. We continued to see each other for about six months. He would fly up from Florida, or wherever he was working, to spend a weekend with me. I had just graduated with my degree from Northern when he arranged for us to meet downstate for Memorial weekend. When I got close to the exit of the town we were meeting at, I glanced over in the lane next to me, at a limousine following me. There he was hanging out of the back window motioning for me to pull over at a rest area. I was stunned. We parked my car at a motel and drove around checking out the area. That was my first ride ever in a limo. I was trying to catch my breath from all of that excitement when he pulled out a big diamond ring and proposed. At the time, I instantly said yes, and felt on top of the world.

Some other unspoken ideas swirled in my head. I knew my ex-husband, with his constant criticism, would make an issue of me being involved with someone while the kids were spending time with me. Morally, looking back, he was right, even though he was seeing other people. Morally, he shouldn't have been unfaithful in our marriage, but men seem to play by different rules. So, that was another factor in me wanting to re-marry. I almost felt a little pressured and that I couldn't say no, after all he had went through to get a limo, buy a beautiful ring, and surprise me. I was in love with him, he was a beautiful man, had a secure job, and was good to me.

My biggest hope and dream was to be in a position financially, with stability, etc. and a home to get custody back of my children. It would all go south as quickly as I rushed into it. My head was stuck in the clouds the first year or so. My second husband's work area encompassed the eastern U.S. It was quite an adventure, travelling around and seeing sights that I never thought were possible. He took me to the Keys in Florida for our honeymoon. We camped in his parents small travel trailer, stayed at the different Keys, and enjoyed watching the most incredible sunsets. Before we reached Miami, we went through Homestead, FL, in 1992. This was shortly after Hurricane Andrew went through and wiped out the town. It was quickly being rebuilt. Stores, homes, school, etc. were already erected when we came through.

As we began our trip to the tropical paradise, we entered the overseas highway, U.S. Highway 1, by way of a series of bridges that connects the islands. The northern Key, Key Largo, brought a song to mind from the 1970s and the movie with Humphrey Bogart both about Key Largo. I don't remember the name of the movie or the song. One of the Keys had miniature, dwarfed deer, no larger than a dog. That was on Key deer. They were protected on that island and had the right-of-way. We stopped to let some cross the road.

From there, we stopped at Marathon to camp. My second ex-husband, like most Floridians, was very water-oriented. He scuba-dived, snorkeled, sailed, and had a love of the water. My fear of water kept me from most of those activities. He had rented a small catamaran and coaxed me out into the ocean, but not too far out. He jumped in with his snorkel to go lobster hunting. Apparently, they use a long "tickle stick," and chase the lobsters out from the rocks and then catch them in a net. I put my snorkel mask on and stuck my head under the turquoise water from the catamaran to watch him. He came up with a couple.

We ended up in Key West. He certainly knew his way around the Keys. He drove me by the author Ernest Hemingway's house. We then went to Jimmy Buffett's Margaritaville Restaurant. I was hoping to see him but alas, he does not perform there or make an appearance very often. We ended the evenings on the boardwalk that had nightly festivals. There were street performers, arts and craft booths, food carts, and many tourists taking in the sights. At dusk, there was a plethora of boats, yachts, dingoes, sailboats, and such, floating near to shore, lit up, waiting to watch some of the most spectacular sunsets you could imagine.

As the sun shined brightly upon my face, it felt good to be alive, and left me with a fresh perspective on life. With his work requiring him to be on the road constantly, the only work I could get was temp work. The temp services were located all over. I worked in a variety of settings from clerical to catering jobs. If I didn't have any work, then I traveled with him on the road.

So, when did it all go bad? It wasn't long before my perky perspective turned into annoyance, longing, and disillusionment. His parents lived in the Daytona Beach area. I did not enjoy waking up to sweat dripping down my face the first thing in the morning. Nor did I care for the stifling hot, wet, heat that barely left you any energy to even walk around. If you left your hot pads at home, then you might very well have gotten second-degree burns from the steering wheel when you got into your car. I burned my ass and bare legs, I don't know how many times, from the hot leather seats. Traffic was fun to drive in too. You couldn't have enough mirrors on your car to watch out for the many lanes of traffic and road-raging drivers, as they about blew your doors off going well over the speed limit.

There are areas in the cities that were drug-ridden and crime-ridden. Drug deals were taking place on the street corners and beaches openly. Prostitutes walked the streets, gangs of motor-cyclers roamed around, and sirens screamed out constantly from police cars, ambulances, and fire-trucks. I was always looking over my shoulder.

When going out for a night on the town, his circle of friends, and everyone else, seemed to dress to the nines. The women looked as though they just walked out of the beauty salon with their hair stiffly sprayed into place, perfect long, painted nails, tip-toeing on their stiletto heels, runway outfits, and accessories to die for. The men were equally impressive with their clean, white tuxedo shirts, dress slacks, polished shoes, gold cufflinks, chains, and rings, and smelling like they had just been dipped in fine, Egyptian oils.

Then there was me, in my K-mart, blue-light specials, primped up as though I had just hopped off Jed Clampet's rocking chair on the back of his truck. I felt a wee bit out of my element. What was I thinking? That I belonged there? I felt like I was under a microscope as they looked me up and down, then dismissed me. I wanted to crawl back into that shell where I felt safe.

The ex tried to get a position with his company where he could settle down but it didn't work out. I was tired of living out of a suitcase. I decided to move back up north and was able to find a job back in the Upper Peninsula (U.P.). It became too impractical to see my children with the costs and distance. I felt relieved to be back in the U.P. My new husband came to see me about every two weeks.

As I became more independent, better educated, had gained life experiences, and felt emotionally stronger, I thought I had become more liberal and open-minded. I thought I would be able to handle the loneliness and be able to trust my husband explicitly. I thought we had the same goals of setting up a home, getting my kids, and having stability in our life.

I started to obsess about little things that he did and made them into big things in my head. This is how the PTSD comes flooding back. I remembered the glamour shot picture of an attractive girl that he kept in his wallet and did not remove until his mother told him to take it out on our wedding day. I thought of the little black book that he did not want to part with that was loaded with girls' names, addresses, and phone numbers in every town he had worked. I was living sober but he liked to drink pretty regularly. He didn't get falling down drunk and it didn't affect his work but he spent time at parties and strip clubs with his friends. That was really starting to bug me, especially if he called late at night and I could hear girl's voices in the background giggling. These were some of the things we argued about on his short visits when he came home. I had a bad feeling where this was going.

The other big bone of contention was his feelings about the U.P. He hated everything about it. My culture shock with Florida was equal to his towards Michigan. He despised the long, cold winters, high unemployment, and boring social life. My idea of fun was the hunting, snowmobiling, snowshoeing, cross-country skiing, ice-fishing, camping, and the wildlife. I lived in fear of the water, the people, traffic, alligators, snakes, and all the other critters that seemed bigger down south.

He tried to adjust to our "Yooper" lifestyle. We bought a snowmobile and I took him out riding. He sat behind me on the sled and I spotted a good-sized snowbank that a front-end loader had made in a parking lot. I was already showing off my ability on the sled by driving at a break neck speed. I gunned it as I started up the hill and yelled for him to "hang on!" He didn't trust me, so he let go, slid off the back, and rolled back down doing somersaults.

He didn't want anything to do with hunting because he was not comfortable around guns and didn't like sitting out in the "freezing cold," even though we were dressed for it. I also thought if he seen the beauty of what "God's country," had to offer, that it would grow on him. We went to Tahquamenon Falls, Lake of the Clouds, Copper Harbor, and other scenic spots but he wasn't all that impressed. Nor was he all that impressed with the Yooper diet of venison and pasties. He was more of a seafood kind of guy.

He was annoyed when we would spend time outdoors while swatting at the mosquitos, deerflies, and picking off woodticks. He watched keenly while we hiked, expecting to break out in a run if a bear, coyote, or wolf should happen to cross our path.

We did have lots of fun times together. He was playful and a good snuggler. Sometimes we would wrestle around. I had taken a couple of years of karate classes and knew just enough to give someone a hard time. I loved Bruce Lee and considered him to be my hero. I wanted to learn his one-inch punch. The ex was a smaller dude, only a few inches taller than me. So, when we wrestled, I could pin him down easily. When he came around a corner, I would startle him by holding my foot sideways, and about 3 inches from his nose. I didn't exactly feel safe with him. I've seen the "shit hit the fan." I know how aggressive people can be. I needed and wanted to feel protected but I didn't feel that way with him.

In one of our last arguments about these differences, he told me that he had "had enough." He told me not to try and make him have to choose between his job and me because there would be no contest. He needed his job. It was my turn to be left, again. I had mixed feelings of wanting a divorce and yet I didn't want to lose him. Once his mind was made up, there was no convincing him that we could fix what was wrong. After many tears, I filed in tribal court, knowing there would be no monetary costs for either of us. We mutually agreed that he would take his things and I would keep mine. He tried to soften the blow by telling me, "let's agree that when we turn 60, that we'll look each other up, no matter who we are with." I could care less if I see him or not. When you are done, you are done. I heard through the grapevine a couple of years later that he had re-married.

The marriage was brief but I do not regret our time together at all. I think we both realized, from our first failed marriages, better to end it sooner rather than years later. When it's over you only spend a long time making each other more miserable.

WANDERING AND PONDERING

My brother Melvin had started college down in Chicago. He was studying Sociology but never completed a degree. That stuck in my mind when I entered college at Northern Michigan University. I wanted to finish what he had started. I wanted to be interested in what he was interested in, so I chose to major in Sociology. I somehow felt a deeper connection to him. I really did enjoy learning about people. They say we go into certain fields that we think will help solve our own problems. I was on a quest to find myself. That was the other motivator when I chose my field of study.

It was intriguing to learn about the behaviors we display in the different stages of life. I could relate with the naivete and immaturity we exhibit in our twenties. I was very gullible and believed everything people told me was gospel. In my thirties I became more serious as I considered my future. My eagerness to get on with life propelled me in a new direction. I wanted a career and knew I was running out of time. I dabbled with a variety of jobs. I became more self-assured in my forties. People couldn't pull the wool over my eyes as easily as before.

I was more intuitive of people and trusted my instincts more. I became very effective at reading body language. God knows I had many years of practice. You can predict what someone is going to do next by their expressions, especially in the eyes, the windows to the soul. The eyes express lust, anger, sadness, and joy.

Some may feel in a defensive mode when they cross their arms. Once during a therapy session, I caught my therapist observing me as I sat across from her. I had my legs crossed but had my hand and part of my arm covering my crotch area. I hadn't realized that I tended to do that frequently. She said that was a common gesture of sex abuse victims. It's almost as if we are protecting the genital area.

The more I learned about myself, the more confidence I felt to express my opinion in a conversation. I spoke up for what I believed in. I learned in college not to speak on an issue unless I knew what I was talking about. By doing research, asking questions, and proving theories leads you down the road to knowledge. I was still looking to find my niche in life, though. I wanted to stuff my life full with meaning.

Again, I needed to be needed. I wanted a partner to share my eagerness for life, someone I had things in common with, before it was too late. After all, look at how quickly life was snatched from my brothers. I knew a partner was out there, somewhere. Meanwhile, I tried to concentrate on myself. My self-defense classes helped to build my confidence also.

I was waitressing at the casino making decent money. There were many good-looking men that made work interesting. I was being flirted with, hit on, and asked out on a number of occasions. I was starting to feel better about myself.

Working for the tribe was an opportunity to be a part of the community. Being around other Native people felt like family. It was a good way to learn about my culture from others that lived their life more traditionally on the reservation. I learned to observe and listen. In our culture, I was told that it was not polite to ask how, what, or why we did things the way we did. You do not learn by simply being told the answer. You must seek it out, watch, and learn by doing. I learned while attending a pow-wow that our people do not wish to have pictures taken of sacred dances or ceremonies. They stress that we should remember in our minds and in our hearts, rather than by pulling out a picture.

While researching in college and through jobs I've held, I discovered the many contributions Native Americans have given to our country. For example, our roads and highways are built on old Indian trails. Our form of government is modeled after the Iroquois Nation, following their councils' way of governing, which had a central power with smaller units. The fundamentals of Boys and Girls Scouts are taken from the Indian way of life, how to build fires, how to read the lay of the land when you are lost, learning survival skills, finding food, etc. We were the first to have a form of tennis shoes, coating the bottom of our feet from rubber trees, and we invented things like tobaggans, canoes, and snowshoes. We grew many of the foods we eat today such as corn, potatoes, squash, and tomatoes. Many states, cities, towns, etc. have Indian names and meanings. Our medicines of today originate from Natives' use of plants.

Our curriculum in school did not address many of these important influences. Any time an issue came up in class concerning Indians, students and even the teacher would look at me, assuming that I must know because I was an Indian. They didn't realize I didn't know much because I was kept from learning anything about my culture. It was times like that when I became quiet, insecure, and felt like an idiot, especially during my college years. I was more comfortable when I was in the company of other Indians. Most of them had similar backgrounds to mine and I didn't feel judged by them.

As I learned about my culture it became obvious to me that there were cultural differences in values and customs in the red versus white world. I understand now, the importance of practicing balance in life, only take what we need, and always give something back. We are the stewards of Mother Earth and must respect all life for future generations. I love the ancient Native American proverb that reminds us "We did not inherit Mother Earth from our ancestors, we are borrowing it from our children."

I had an opportunity to go into a woman's sweat lodge, and it was a beautiful experience. One must prepare properly before partaking in this ceremony by being clean and sober. Instructions are given of what to expect before entering. We sat on cedar boughs, took turns praying to the four directions, all of the animals, and for all of the people. The "grandfathers" (red-hot rocks) were brought in one at a time, by the fire tender, usually with a pitchfork. They glowed in the dark wigwam as we splashed water on them after each prayer. It became so hot, you found yourself with your nose on the ground trying to find cool air to breathe. If you felt faint, you yelled, "door," and the flap was lifted for you to exit. You try to get past your weaknesses, though, and offer it up as suffering for our people. There is more to it than this, but suffice to say that it leaves the person feeling cleansed, released, and stronger.

I wanted to learn what I could about what we had missed out on by not being raised by our biological parents. This was the missing link of my identity. Why was I born? What was the Creator's plan for me? If everything happens for a reason, what was the reason I went through what I had? The same questions reappeared in my life at different times.

One of my more important teachings was regarding eagle feathers. Our people believe that the eagle takes our prayers up to the Creator. Eagles are considered to be sacred and their feathers are used in ceremonies and at times in the regalia worn. It is an honor to receive an eagle feather. It must be earned by doing something selfless, honorable, brave, or something for your people. It is federal law that Native Americans are the only people legally protected to possess eagle feathers. Sometimes I go looking for eagle feathers by the water, or areas where I've seen them. There are times when I do find some. I've been told that if you are meant to find one, you will. Some people may go through their whole life and not find any.

All of my experiences have given me a better sense of "self." I am more comfortable in my skin. I've learned more about my culture. I understand what my family has gone through. I now know why and how things turned out the way they did.

As I've rehashed my life, I find myself having a new perspective than I did when I first began my story. We do not have a choice but to walk in both worlds. The European values and customs may be most influential in the life we live today. However, the American Indian values and way of life from the past have made an even bigger impact than most realize.

SISTERLY LOVE

My sister's life paralleled mine. She was the only one who could truly understand and relate with what I had been through. We had both suffered the same abuses and losses. We have always tried to be there for each other when in need. She had two failed marriages also. Today we both have health issues brought about, I feel, from the trauma we have lived through.

She also had four children and we got together often. I don't know how we got our 8 kids all in the same car to go and do things together, but we did. Like me, she had three boys and 1 girl. Her children were practically the same ages as mine. If it hadn't been for her being with me while growing up, I really don't think that I could have tolerated some of what I did.

We were reminiscing about old times one night. She had came for a visit and brought one of my nephews. She told her son, matter-of-factly, "my sister raised me." I guess I never knew she felt that way. It was good to hear and it made me happy. I didn't know if she realized how much I tried to protect her and give her to make up for the family we lost. That kind of bond cannot be broken. Although we both love our youngest sister, that bond is not as strong because we weren't raised with her. Perhaps we even resented the fact that she was the only one our mother took when she left. It felt like she was more important to her than we were.

Sis got to spend more time with our biological mother than I did. She moved to Milwaukee for awhile and lived with her. Our mother got to enjoy some of her grandchildren. I went down there a few times to visit them. Our mother told us many stories that gave us insight into her life.

She said after living with our father and taking all of that abuse, she swore to herself that she would never let that happen again. The next man in her life tried to knock her around one night when they were drinking together. She said that when she hit the floor, she spotted a wine bottle on the coffee table, grabbed it, smashed it on the table, and when he came toward her she rammed it into his knee. He had to go to the hospital to get stitched up. Another time when he pissed her off, she waited until he passed out on the floor, then she knew she could have her revenge. She said he was lying on a rug, so she rolled him up in it and tried to light it on fire.

I knew whom we got our spunk from. She was babysitting for sis one day, but had to go out for an errand, so she had her neighbor lady across the hall watch the kids. When she got back, the neighbor started bitching at her, pointing and wagging her finger in her face about the grandkids. She was mad that they wouldn't drink their milk and thought it was wasteful. All of our kids, like us, had lactose intolerance. My mother told her that she'd better get that finger out of her face or she was going to snap it off. She just kept on so my mother grabbed her by the neck and started punching her in the face. She had to go to court for assault.

Yes, she was a wild one. She told us about another incident. She had left the bar after a night of drinking and went home. Her nephew called her and told her she had better come down there because some lady was talking shit about her. She grabbed her handgun, walked in, and went up to the booth where they were all sitting. She said there was a bunch of beer bottles on the table. She swiped them all off the table with one arm while brandishing her gun in the other hand. They all dove under the table. Pointing it towards the woman, she asked, "Now, what was it you were saying about me?" She told the cops she had left her clip at home and just wanted to scare them.

Sis and I got to know my Uncle Ira and my Aunt Betty, my mother's brother and sister, and their kids, cousins on my mom's side. They were all just as much fun as the relatives on our dad's side of the family. They treated us like we had all grown up together, even though we were more like strangers. Sis became closer to our younger sister while living in Milwaukee. She has three great kids that she pretty much raised on her own. I'm sure she went through her own torment being separated from her older siblings.

Our mother told us that she had two more daughters with Dick Jackson, the man she lived with in Milwaukee, but that she gave them up at birth. She also told us that she had another son that had been born between sis and me. She said that she had split up from our father for awhile and she was with another man that she had a child with. She had given him up at birth, also. After our brothers died, she had wrote a letter to the state and tried to track him down. She could not get any more information about what had happened to him. She only knew that his name was Michael, he would have been born around 1960. We did some research too, but could not find out anything. When she passed away, she still longed to find him. It was her dying wish. We have taken up that desire and would like to find him, that is, if he is even still alive.

When mother retired from Briggs & Stratton, she had a stroke that left her partially paralyzed. Soon after, she had to go on a dialysis machine. She moved back up to Watersmeet and lived on her own for awhile nearer to family. Both of my sisters eventually moved back up north also. We got together with mom often in Watersmeet and it was like coming home again. We had finally come full circle. Our relatives told us how much they had missed us and wanted to know what we had been up to all of these years. They told me how proud they were of me for finishing college. All of their love felt real, and it warmed my heart and my soul.

Northern Michigan University had a minority program for the Black, Native, and Hispanic students. The multi-cultural program provided individual tutoring, study groups, had part-time employment on campus, and they sponsored a number of events. They hosted a pow-wow, talent show, and an international food fest, to name a few. I participated in some of the programming while I attended college. The strong minority women, who ran the program, provided the kind of confident leadership I hoped one day to emulate. The encouragement and camaraderie from other minority students helped me to stay in school and complete my degree. It wasn't easy trying to concentrate on my studies while going through a divorce. However, the day finally arrived for my graduation. I did it, and I felt proud for completing it. After accomplishing a degree, as a scholar, we hold a responsibility to our fellow mankind. By sharing our knowledge with those who want to hear what we've learned, facilitating understanding where we can, and by encouraging others that they can be anything they want to be, helps to make the world a little better place. We need more of building each other up rather than tearing others down.

My sis and I keep in touch and see each other often. Although we are 4 hours away from each other, the miles do not keep us apart. She is a true Yooper, like me, and returned home. She is fortunate to be in closer proximity to her grandchildren than I am. I know she is busy spending time and having fun with them. I realized that I was not the best role model for her. She always said how she looked up to me. Truth be known, there is much I admire about her. She has always been feisty, straightforward and real, compassionate, giving, and determined. I remember her working two or three jobs all at the same time to support her kids. She was always there for me in every way.

We had our little spats along the way, like siblings do, but our time together brings me so much joy. Okay, there were two, bad, knock-down-drag-out fights, but we got over it. Mostly though, our time together is spent laughing until we are crying. In our suffering together, we held each other up, and trudged on. Our love for each other has formed a bond that cannot be broken.

GROUNDHOG DAY

Remember that movie Groundhog Day with Bill Murray where he kept living the same day over and over? That seemed to be my life story. I would soon be meeting my next ex-husband.

When I came back to Baraga, from Florida in the summer of 1995, I got a job at the tribe's casino, as a cocktail waitress. Indian gaming had become quite popular. We were fairly busy and tips were decent. It was good to be amongst old friends again. Life was less hectic and quieter in the U.P. than the rat race in Florida.

I had missed the simple life and the beauty of Lake Superior. The Ojibway also referred to her as Gitchee Gumee, or Big Water. As in Henry Longfellow's poem of Hiawatha, "By the shore of Gitchee Gumee," my ancestors too, paddled in birch bark canoes along the lake.

Baraga is located on the western shore, while L'Anse sits across the bay, on the eastern shore of the lake. As the sun rises over the peak of Mount Arvon, one of the highest elevations in the state, the locals are awakened to the sweet chirping and singing of many different species of birds. I also loved gazing at the bright light of the moon, especially when it is full and its reflection shimmers off the water. I had missed the serenity of being in the woods and watching the wildlife scampering about.

You have to be quite vigilant about dodging white-tail deer on the roads. Usually, where there is one crossing the road, there is bound to be another right behind it. Every now and again you might catch a glimpse of black bear, raccoons, fox, porcupines, etc. On some quiet nights just outside of town you can hear the yipping of coyotes. They are quickly silenced with one howl from the wolf. More recently moose have been introduced in the area and their population has really grown. Some have even seen the more elusive cougar.

While I was gone, though, things had been brewing in tribal politics. I wasn't home more than a couple of months when a hostile take-over occurred in the tribe. My college education was about to be put to good use. I was just trying to mind my own business because I figured I didn't know the whole story of both sides, but I got dragged into it.

It is said that Native Americans have learned well from the White man. As a result of becoming acculturated, we somehow lost sight of our cultural values that teach us to take care of each other. Rather than feast or famine together, some tribal councils become corrupted by power. In order to compete in the White world, we take on the new values of, "every man for himself." Gaming has brought a lot of revenue to the reservations and the decisions on how to "spread the wealth," sometimes causes conflict within the tribe.

The Keweenaw Bay Tribe, (KB) was one of the first in the country to introduce gaming. Tribal Chairman Dakota had always been respected and considered a man of the people. Mr. Dakota originally opened a gambling establishment in his garage, testing the waters on the parameters of the sovereignty issue. Federal regulations were quickly implemented for Indian gaming. Gaming was allowed to go forward but only if was controlled by the tribe and not by an individual. Up until then, the only person benefiting from profits was Fred Dakota. He was living a lucrative lifestyle and in a small community people took notice. It is difficult to imagine that Mr. Dakota achieved that success without using tribal resources for his own personal gain. At the very least, I would think the tribal attorney had to give legal advice as to how to proceed.

KB tribal member, Rose Edwards has written a succinct account of the events that led up to a hostile take-over and the unscrupulous incidents that took place during the approximate two-year stand off. She has earned recognition writing about this matter. It can be found on the Internet at:

baragarose.tripod.com.

The discontent grew when it became obvious positions of authority were being abused, nepotism ruled, and outrageous salaries were being paid to those with questionable qualifications. The disdain grew and was directed at the few families and their supporters that held the power. The unfairness and inequality of their actions toward others had reached a tipping point.

Some tribal members that wanted to do something to change the situation, ran for tribal council at the next election, and won. Mr. Dakota and the other incumbents that lost refused to give up their seats. Mr. Dakota's son's position as tribal judge was also in jeopardy as an opponent tied with him. They schemed to nullify the election by saying that tribal members, who were not eligible to vote, had voted. This was a voting list that had been approved and validated for years. They went down the list of names and the bulk of which they could determine had voted against them was expelled from the voting process.

As you can imagine the purged voters were not going to take it lying down. The opposition faction went into the tribal administrative building in the middle of the night, and barricaded themselves in. They called themselves, Fight for Justice, also known as FFJ. These were brave men, women, and some young people who chose to make a stand. When the administration came in the following morning, all hell broke loose. Support from both sides also showed up, demands and threats were made, and the old council was told to leave. On their way out, protestors checked their vehicles to make sure they did not take public records. Mr. Dakota summoned tribal police from other reservations in the state, for backup, and the standoff began. Things were about to get very nasty. It started out intending to be a non-violent protest of civil disobedience but soon became an out of control battle to the bitter end.

I was bewildered when I heard about what had happened. One woman asked me where I stood on the situation. I told her I didn't know enough about it to choose a side. She told me that I should care because my name was on the list that was not allowed to vote. With that challenge, I began to ask questions from both sides to get a better understanding of the conflict.

After hearing about what Dakota had done, I felt as indignant and enraged as the protestors did. It was an easy choice to side with the underdogs. The other side had the scales tipped in their favor. They seemed to be untouchable. The community became split down the middle. Those who dared to speak up against Dakota and the council were getting fired from their jobs. They faced trumped up charges in tribal court, had long sentences or heavy fines imposed, were evicted from tribal housing, denied services, banned from the casino, intimidated by people, threatened by social services to have their children taken away, and stripped of their voting rights. Naturally the "Freddie's" were getting away with harassing, intimidating, shooting at the building, brandishing guns, and were rewarded with the good jobs, good pay, while not having to face any consequences for domestic violence cases, DUI's, and other crimes that they were involved in.

When it hit the news media, some of the outside tribal councils ordered their police to return to their reservations, a couple of other tribal police units stayed. In addition, Dakota had hired a private security service that was mostly made up of non-Indians. He replaced the terminated, tribal police officers that refused to arrest some of their relatives on the FFJ side, with non-Indian officers also. Some of his supporters who were known local drunks were paid, either with booze or money, to go and harass protestors at "the compound." One person with the FFJ group had his house shot up while he was away. Antagonists from Fred's side would do drive-by shootings toward the building.

The Federal Bureau of Investigation had jurisdiction over felonious crimes on the reservation. The Bureau of Indian Affairs, (BIA) also had jurisdiction over the tribal police. These agencies refused to get involved and referred to it as an "internal problem." The official, BIA investigator that they had sent down was seen out having cocktails at the casino with the Dakota side. Dakota became outraged that federal authorities would not do his bidding. He even went so far in an interview, as to say, "if they want a body, we'll give them a body."

The members of the occupation were all sober people. No alcohol was allowed on the premises. The compound was just outside of town by a couple of miles. It had two entrances. One was off US 41 highway at the bottom of the hill, and one at the top of the hill located off a county road, but within the reservation boundary. FFJ members took turns, in shifts, to watch the two entrances. How no one ever got shot is a miracle.

I started writing letters to the editor in the local paper critiquing the politics of the tribe. The local weekly newspaper, *The L'Anse Sentinel*, enthusiastically covered the details as they occurred. The paper was often bought out at the stands. Tribal members passed it around to those eagerly waiting to catch up on the latest drama. The paper couldn't even escape the oppression of Dakota's regime. They attempted to trample on the rights of the press by threatening to sue them for slander and libel.

Several people at work told me that I had better "watch my ass, because they were gunning for me." They were looking for any reason to fire me. They also figured by taking peoples income away, leaving them with no way to support their family, that they would "shut up," and not bad-mouth the council. It did work on quite a few people. It also had the opposite effect on some people.

I was three minutes late for work one night at the casino, and my supervisor was going to give me a three-day lay off. It was a wintry, snowy day; most employees had called in saying that they couldn't make it because the roads were so bad. They used this as an opportunity to put me in my place for writing articles that humiliated them. So when I was called into the back and told of my reprimand, I responded that he could take the job and shove it up his ass; I quit. I threw my nametag and little apron at him and out the door I went. I knew it was coming, but it still upset me.

Finally, due to the violent tone that the insurrection had taken, some tribal members contacted the American Indian Movement (AIM) in Minneapolis to ask for help. They told them of the heightened violence and of their fear that someone was going to be killed. AIM came and many supporters followed from all over the country. At that time, I did not know what the Movement represented, exactly. I knew that they fought for Native American rights but I was not aware of their history, tactics, or impact they had made for our people.

They spoke to both factions, wanting to give everyone the opportunity to defend their beliefs and actions. They interviewed victims that had been fired, kicked out of housing, arrested, intimidated, harassed or threatened in any way. Dakota's people were surprised when they had a microphone or tape recorder shoved in their face at the most inopportune moment. They were confronted on the spot with a barrage of questions about their behavior and actions. AIM leaders, or Grand Council, took their findings to the media and spoke out against the corruption, stripping of voting rights, loss of basic human rights, and the violence. I remember seeing an interview of Fred on television. They asked him to respond to AIM's findings. Fred said, "Well who's AIM?" He quickly spun his head to look behind his left shoulder. He then said, "Who's AIM to be telling anybody anything?" He immediately snapped his head back over his right shoulder. It would have been just like an AIM representative to be standing right behind him with their arms folded. They would have asked, "What did you just say?"

Having access to the administrative records, FFJ and AIM worked together gathering the necessary documents that were incriminating enough to move forward to the proper authorities. AIM brought new vitality, pride, confidence, and encouragement to the protesters. They quickly sorted "the men from the boys." They told everyone, "if you are afraid of getting fired, getting beat up, or going to jail, then LEAVE, we can't use you." They lectured and scolded, but told it like it was to everyone present. They said that the time was now to work together, stick together, don't back down, and stand up for what you believe in. Most importantly, they advised, the only way to make it happen was to get back to our traditional values of our culture and practice our customs.

This is where I met my third husband. He came to Baraga to help the protesters soon after it began. He was a big man, with a native ancestry, even though he didn't look it, with his blond ponytail and light-blue eyes. I thought he had good looks, nice complexion, good teeth, nice smile, and a loud, low booming voice. He was a former marine, boxer, and had a lengthy history with the law. This was the perfect background for someone with an aggressive personality. He did not hesitate to confront anyone, even if they had a weapon in their hand. Here was someone that didn't even know these people, but refused to stand by while innocent people were being terrorized. There was no one he feared, or who could threaten him, or that he felt intimidated by. He had a very much, "in-your-face," kind of attitude. I thought to myself, wow, I wished I could be more like that in my life. I would have stood up to my father, to my ex, to the bullies who talked down to me. We started going out after getting to know each other at the compound.

I was so impressed that this stranger would risk his life, literally, to protect these people. Most of the men could protect themselves, but there were many elderly, handicapped, and youngsters that stayed at the compound. The individuals who went in during the night originally were very brave. Equally brave, were the supporters who stood outside the doors, the building, and at the entrances, facing the uncertain dangers that came their way.

I wrote furiously to the editor almost weekly. People wanted to read who was getting ripped into or who was ripping into me. I let the truth fly because I really did have nothing left to lose, and my newest beau was not one to let anyone pick on me. They dared not to say or do anything to me, lest they face his wrath. I felt protected and secure, as if I had my own private bodyguard.

I tried to bring awareness to the nepotism, hypocrisy, abuse of their positions, the lost cultural value of caring for everyone, the oppression, and loss of basic human rights, through my articles. I was also thinking that maybe I finally found my niche. I didn't just complain or incite, but offered examples, solutions, compromises, and voiced the wishes of the people.

The situation came to a boiling point when Fred's side had planned to take back the premises and arrest all of those involved. He had new, non-Indian tribal police replacements that would not hesitate to take his directives. There were still one or two other tribes that allowed their tribal police to stay and assist. Fred's side also had his spies or snitches that played both sides.

Rumors flew as to when Fred would make his move. The police's every move was being watched also. There were instances when tribal police car tires had been flattened. No names were ever mentioned and for all we knew, Fred's people could have been doing things of this nature and blaming the protesters, in order to set them up. At times, stories were told with misinformation to catch the snitches that would take any info they heard back to the other side.

Somehow, information was obtained, from a reliable source, of the date for the next attempted raid. The protestors at the compound readied themselves. As what often happened when push came to shove, a small group was left to face the onslaught. The tribal police arrived early that morning fully dressed in riot gear, billy clubs, and carrying assault rifles. Three or four police cars came and blocked the top entrance while three police cars blocked the bottom entrance. They gave us three minutes to evacuate the premises. When no one moved, they began by firing tear gas. Some of the protesters wearing gloves, responded by picking up the gas canisters, like a hot potato, and threw them back at the police. They ducked behind their squad cars as a volley of rocks was hurled their way. Some of the police pulled out their shotguns and rifles, laid over the hoods of their cars, and pointed them at the protesters. The protesters stood in defiance in the face of the threat, holding clubs and rocks.

It was a half-hearted attempt by both sides. Neither side wanting to go to the extreme but willing to do what they had to do. Thankfully, no shots were fired, and the police, not wanting to escalate the situation any further, finally withdrew. It was an exhaustive day for both sides. The stress and strain showed on our faces. At the same time, it demonstrated the determination of just how far both sides were willing to go for what they believed in.

The lengthy investigation by federal authorities finally culminated with a warrant for Fred's arrest. He threw a lot of money around the Marquette area, such as the Children's Museum and other places in hopes of buying a "not guilty" verdict. He even hired protesters to demonstrate in downtown Marquette. The judge ordered that the trial be moved downstate. To Fred's dismay, he was prosecuted for tax evasion and bribery in federal court. The takeover finally wound down. It has taken the tribe years to heal as the community finally came back together. Fred eventually served his sentence and later, surprisingly, was re-elected back on the tribal council. Tribal politics are just as cut-throat as it is in our nation's government. Tribal councils often times take on non-Indian values in order to have a seat at the table in the world of politics.

My soon-to-be third husband and I got caught up in the moment. We were thrown together in a desperate and dangerous situation. I was surprised, after only three weeks of dating; he was already telling me he loved me. I told him that he didn't even really know me. He had started talking marriage early on in the relationship. Again, I felt hesitant and pressured on one hand, but had to agree with him on the other hand. He did treat me good, life was short, and we both felt committed to each other, so why not try it again? Six months later we got married.

My dream of a professional career was pretty much doomed. I was now officially blackballed for my radical opinions. Who wants a whistle-blower to come in and expose any misappropriations or have their dirty laundry aired? I began bartending part time in the small town I had moved to with husband number three.

The first summer that we met, the Forest Service was offering a wildland fire-fighting training in Watersmeet. I had a cousin that had been fighting wildfire for a number of years. He convinced his sister, a friend of mine, and me that we could do the work. The three of us attended the week-long training and became certified. I was dispatched to my first fire that summer out to Bailey, CO. The work was hard but the paycheck was well worth it.

I truly thought that it didn't matter to me what possessions we had or didn't have. I could give anyone a chance with me if I was treated with respect and shown love. As hard as he fought, for people he didn't even know, I thought he would work even harder at building a nice life for us. I believed in him when he told me his work was steady and that he was always busy. He seemed to be motivated. I began to notice that as much as his father frustrated him and annoyed him, that he had similar personality traits, as his father did. It was in the genes. His dad also raised him when his parents got divorced. He could be just as bull-headed as his father was when challenged. Life had made him "set in his ways," at a young age. He may not like to admit it, but he liked to exaggerate and stretch the truth often, in conversations.

I liked to laugh and he had a sense of humor that would not stop. He was very quick-witted and could add-on to whatever was said and turn it into hilarity. So, he was fun to be around. He was very perceptive of people and could see them for what they were. He had what was needed to become an activist, outspokenness, no fear, and no filter. We became sanctioned by AIM and started an AIM-Michigan Chapter. We were busy for awhile travelling around where Native groups requested our assistance. Tribal members from the Saginaw Tribe were fighting similar issues that had happened at Keweenaw Bay, so we went there. The AIM-Arizona Chapter also called us to come out and rally with them against a corrupt tribal council. Some of our time there was spent helping needy families and a Native veteran. We advocated for him and were able to get him to the appropriate resources that could help his circumstances.

Vernon Bellecourt, one of the leaders from AIM, asked us to attend a protest that was being held at the International Bridge, near Detroit. It was regarding the Jay Treaty, which concerned Indigenous rights of working and trading across international borders. He also wanted us to check into a group of people calling themselves AIM-Michigan but hadn't been sanctioned by them. Friends and supporters followed us down. We were very outnumbered by this other group and felt as though something was going to break out, and so we decided to leave. On the way out, we took a wrong turn, on the Canadian side. All of a sudden, out of no where, police surrounded us. They were in a paddy wagon, on motorcycles, squad cars, a helicopter, and snipers on the roof, all pointing guns at us. Our friends in the car behind started taking pictures. My husband's truck had large AIM shields on the doors. It read, "American Indian Movement" and had the AIM logo. There were four of us in the truck.

They told us all, over a loudspeaker, "Put your hands up!" We immediately obeyed. I didn't know what was about to happen and it was scarey. They made the men get out, hands up, lean on the hood, patted them down, and then let us go. I don't know if they were expecting a riot to break out, or what, but that was freaky.

I had always been a scrapper, while growing up, but wanted to learn more about self-defense. I continued to attend karate class. I would soon be using what I had learned. There was some bad blood between another woman and me. She was on the "Fred side." One day, when we saw each other and after exchanging insults, she grabbed my hair and it was on. I hit her until she let go of my hair. She called the tribal police on me and pressed charges against me in tribal court. Tribal court only had the authority to hear misdemeanors. The tribal judge was an elected position. Judges usually did not have a law background, you were not afforded a public defender, and Fred's son just happened to sit on the bench.

They were more than happy to get even with me for all that I wrote about them in the paper. I had never been in trouble with the law so this was my first offense. I was incarcerated for two weeks, had a $1000.00 fine, and six months of probation. Because of this incident, I was unable to attend my oldest son's wedding, which caused a lot of pain for him as well as me. The tribal warrant was only legitimate on the reservation. His marriage ceremony was within these boundaries. Intentions were to arrest me at his wedding. I wasn't about to let them ruin the wedding, so I stayed away. It was a political prosecution like so many others on the Fight for Justice side.

When the takeover was finally over, my marriage felt like it was also winding down. They say when people get together during times of traumatic events that when the trauma stops, there is time to re-evaluate what you have. We tried to keep the momentum going by reaching out to other Native people from different reservations. Our need to help others was something that we had in common. He had proven what a great leader he could be. He instilled confidence in people when there was fear. It was a thankless job. We had so little money but still tried to do what we could. The threat of jail time, bonds, fines, and warrants seemed to hang over our heads. We had made a lot of enemies. Our desire to put our asses on the line soon fizzled out.

Our circle of friends were Natives that practiced the traditional ways. We were grateful for what they taught us about our culture. Our standard of living seemed to be sliding backwards. There was little work for him. My part-time job didn't pay much. Our trailer house was deteriorating from age. We had to deal with frozen water pipes every winter. Snakes, mice, spiders, were starting to infest the trailer. These were all of my phobias. I realized that living this kind of life didn't bother him. I couldn't deal with it any longer. I became resentful and felt that I had worked too hard to try and have a better life. I learned along the way that you can only change yourself. Some women, like myself, always think we can change a man. I thought that if he loved me, he'd change.

As what always happened, when circumstances reminded me of my past hard times, PTSD comes on, takes over, and there is no stopping it. I began to obsess, fret, and tried to fight the feeling of wanting to run away again. I knew things wouldn't change and might even get worse. I had to take control of my life for my own sanity. I was worn down from watching his anger issues, low frustration level, and complacency that came between us. Again, I needed more. I wanted us both to be all that we could be and meet each other in the middle. He was rough around the edges but had a big heart. That's what else I loved about him. I can take some of the blame for our marriage going wrong but I will not take all of the blame. It came down to wanting different things out of life.

It was about this time an opportunity came along for me. A friend told me that a construction project in Marquette was looking to hire minorities. They needed laborers. I figured with my fire-fighting background that I would be able to handle a physical job. Between that job, which paid well, and fire-fighting in the summer, my income improved.

I knew that at my age, I might have one more move in me to start over. I filed for divorce and moved to Marquette where I was working and already in a graduate program at NMU. I let him have everything, which wasn't a whole lot. This wasn't my first rodeo. I didn't have much but what I did have was mine. I finished my

Masters degree in Public Administration.

I had struck up a good friendship with his sister while we were married. I was so happy that she didn't hold anything against me when we divorced. She continues to be a cherished friend. We are the same age and have a lot in common. Her brother was able to find love again and I am happy for him.

JACK OF ALL TRADES/MASTER OF ONE

I'm considered to be an elder now in my tribe at 55 years of age. As I look back at my sordid life and recall my work history, I make note of the many jobs I've held. The many setbacks I've had to deal with in my personal life has really impacted my job security, or lack thereof.

Our adopted parents taught us the responsibility of chores when we were old enough to perform them. In hindsight, it was good for us. It teaches a child that everyone in the family needs to contribute for the betterment of the whole. They never paid us an allowance. Instead, they told us that if we wanted or needed something, we were to let them know and they would get it for us.

My work history started with babysitting. I was pretty good at saving my money, even at the young age of thirteen. My parents were such control freaks that they wouldn't let us spend the money we earned on just any whim. Once I turned 14, as I discussed previously, the tribe hired me for summer work. It only paid minimum wage but it gave me a work ethic. Actually, I have to give credit where credit is due. My adopted parents demonstrated that if you work hard, good things would come to you in life.

I also enjoyed the social aspect of working. I made girlfriends that were also hired with me. We enjoyed flirting with the boys. The summer work added to my little bank account, and I was able to save up about $800.00. It felt rewarding having the responsibility of buying my own school clothes. It was nice having spending money for dances, games, shooting pool, snacks, or buying little gifts for the family also.

My high school classes of typing and shorthand gave me an edge for clerical jobs at the tribe. I maintained good grades in these classes. Playing the piano gave me the nimble fingers needed to be able to type fast. I had a good job doing clerical work just out of high school. It was a good job until I had a bad experience with my boss. Some co-workers were going out for drinks up to Houghton, MI. I had too much to drink and did not use common sense. My boss was giving me a ride home but made a little detour down a back road. He tried groping me in the car before finally taking me home. The next day, I up and quit, and never told them why. Alcoholism is a disease that wreaks havoc in people's lives. It sure did in mine.

After sobering up, my next job was as an office manager for the county counseling services where court-ordered people were sent as part of their sentences. Some clients came for counseling on their own in an effort to improve their lives. My boss was morbidly overweight, a passive/aggressive weasel of a woman, who started to embezzle money from the office. I was responsible for depositing the money in the bank when I discovered a discrepancy. I wasn't sure how to handle it. I told one of the counselors and a board member. They fired her soon after I reported it. I didn't want to be blamed and she seemed to be setting me up to take the fall. I never stole a thing in my life, except for that pair of underwear. I worked there for about two years when I was married to my kids' dad. The pay was decent money. I quit that job for a better paying job.

I was hired at the public school for a cultural enrichment program for the native students. The position included developing cultural curriculum and teaching native crafts. I learned a lot about native culture from this job. I had a great supervisor to work for. She was very supportive and respectful. This job was a pilot program and was funded on an annual basis. I learned how to do some aspects of grant writing while working there. She sent me to many national training seminars with renowned speakers in Indian Education. I gained new insight into the more traditional ways of teaching native students. This job was only for the school year and was dependent on securing the grant.

The kid's dad still hadn't obtained a steady job. The next job I secured was with the tribe again. This was another pilot program and grant-funded.

The pay was slightly higher than what I was previously doing. I was able to save on gas money because I didn't have to travel as far for work. It was working with single mothers teaching social skills and parenting classes. A psychologist came down from Houghton, who was a white lady, to head up the program. I was her co-facilitator for the group classes. I did this for one year. The next year I had to resign because my personal life was in chaos. I was getting divorced and moving to Marquette to enter college full-time.

I had been working and taking college classes part-time. By then I had completed an Associates degree in liberal arts and was transferring to Northern Michigan University (NMU). When I met with my supervisor and told her I had to quit, she went off on me and read me the riot act. She told me the program had invested a lot of time with me, getting the program off the ground. She told me I was being selfish and thoughtless. I choked back tears, not knowing how to respond, and felt like a wimp for not standing up for myself. I still did not do well with confrontations. She reminded me of my ex-husband, putting me in my place, and talking to me as if I was worthless.

The tribe didn't have a problem with the situation at all. They understood that things come up that aren't planned and people switched jobs all the time. They still deal with turnover in staff quite often. They know how to roll with it and don't let it impede their governing.

While attending Northern, I worked part-time as a program specialist with the minority office. I learned quite a bit from other native students from around the state that attended NMU. It also enriched my understanding of other cultures. I enjoyed working with the Hispanic and Black students. We all encouraged each other. I had a lot of fun and found the events that we sponsored to be quite enriching.

After completing my bachelor's degree, I obtained a position with another local tribe in the U.P. It was doing social work in sexual abuse cases that were being federally prosecuted. I thought this would be a good fit for me. I ran into trouble with my co-worker. He started to sexually harass me to the point that it was hard to get our work done. His constant eye-balling me and sexual innuendoes were creeping me out. By this time, I was able to assert myself and asked to speak with him at work, in private. I told him it was very distracting, that it made me uncomfortable the way he was looking at me and the inappropriate comments he made. He took this as a rejection and then tried to sabotage my work with our supervisor. He started to meet with our supervisor without me and suggested to her that he should be appointed over me, given his higher Master's Degree.

I was married to my second husband at the time, but he was working in Florida. I rented a house in the Soo (Sault Ste. Marie, MI) and lived there alone. My intention was to move my kids down when I was settled. Unfortunately, this job only lasted three months.

I filed a sexual harassment complaint against him with the personnel department. He even showed up at my house one night uninvited with his young daughter. I tried to discuss it with my supervisor. She told me she wanted my complaint in writing. To make a long story short, the department head saw me as the trouble-maker, would not take me seriously, and wanted to fire me. I met with another woman that told me he had acted the same way with her. I asked her if she would support me in my complaint but she said that she could not. She said that given the tribal politics, it would go no where, and she would be the one fired for being a trouble maker. After a big stink, many meetings in the chain of command that went no where, I finally resigned. I later learned that he was fired six months later for doing the same harassing behavior to another co-worker.

I went back down to Florida to be with my second husband. I lived in Florida for a short time, and the only work I could find there was temp work. I was sent to various locations and did menial jobs such as typing, answering phones, or catering set up.

I had a whistle-blower attitude that made me lose many jobs. People don't like conflict. I'm not one to look the other way, sweep it under the rug, or remain with the status quo when there is an element of wrongdoing. Some administrators must think it is too difficult of a process to address the problem and work out a solution. Why not fix the problem and make the program more effective?

At this juncture, things were on a down-hill slide in my second marriage. I knew that if we divorced that I would move back to Baraga. My kids were there, along with some friends and a few relatives. I always seemed to find some kind of work up north.

There were other part-time jobs that I did in my past. I was a census taker at one point. I worked with juvenile delinquents on some week-ends. The tribe wanted adults to watch some kids who had gotten into trouble and were awaiting court. It was similar to being mentors to the teenagers. I also did some court advocacy work.

After my second divorce, I found myself back in my hometown, waittessing at the casino. When the "hostile take-over" happened, many involved lost their jobs, I was one of them. I met and married my third husband and we began our activist work. I did some part-time bar-tending where we lived in Republic, MI, about an hour east of Baraga.

I was asked to be a featured speaker at a law forum Northern Michigan University was sponsoring. The theme was on "street justice." They knew of our involvement at the KB rez, and because I was an alumnus from NMU, they were interested in having our perspective. I was honored that they asked me and I graciously accepted. I prepared my speech and went over it until I knew it like the back of my hand.

As the day approached, many factors entered into the equation that almost made me cancel the speech. The Tribe had caught wind that I was going to speak and didn't want me recounting the specifics of the takeover that would make them look bad. They called the President of the university and asked him why they would let a "criminal," like me, speak. They were referring to my assault charges. They also threatened that if they were going to allow me to speak, they would not be donating any more money to the university. The public university, with its atmosphere for free speech, was not deterred by this threat. Then they started the rumor that if I spoke, the tribal police were going to exercise their warrant out on me for the assault charge. Of course, they had no jurisdiction off reservation land for the misdemeanor charges, but they tried everything they could think of to prevent me from speaking.

Campus security also heard of the potential ruckus and decided to show up, just in case things got out of hand. The public television channel from the university also thought it might be newsworthy, so they showed up also. They were in the back of the room setting up their camera and big lights. By then I was starting to get a panic attack. Luckily, the audience was a small crowd, maybe 30 people in attendance. My daughter and my mother showed up to support me and sat directly in the front row. As I looked at them, I realized I would have to scrap a portion of my speech concerning why and how I got involved in social justice. I didn't want to embarrass my daughter by talking about my divorce from her dad and being on my own. I also didn't want to hurt my mother's feelings by discussing our life in poverty and our family breaking up, so I scratched that part of my speech.

I'll tell you what, with law enforcement in the back of the room, the threat of being arrested, bright lights and the television crew recording, family members and all eyes in the room on me, my mind went blank and my mouth went dry. It was all I could do to keep from running out of that room screaming. I opened my mouth to talk but all that would come out was "ah, um, ah."

I started out by saying how I wanted to use my education to be a voice for those who couldn't speak up for themselves. I finally told them the reasons why I was so uncomfortable giving this speech. I said that it might flow more easily if I started by fielding questions. They asked many questions and I was able to elaborate and give them more information. I somehow relaxed, got through it, and was satisfied with how it went. Afterward, my mother told me how proud she was of me, but she said if I would have talked about how I got my first dress she would have slid right under her chair.

I continued to be an emergency wildland fire fighter. Of all the jobs that I've done, fire fighting was the most rewarding. I continued to fight fire until

I got too old to climb mountains. When I said, "Master of One," I, by no means, am calling myself a master of fire fighting. I am referring to the one job that I've held the longest and loved the most. I started in 1996 but ended up taking two years off when I went to graduate school. In 2012, I had to give it up because my knees were getting shot. I was slow climbing and couldn't risk being a detriment to the crew.

At one time, the KB tribe considered the fire crew to be a valuable asset. There was not much notice given when we got dispatched, but their jobs would be waiting for them when they returned home. That is not the case anymore.

I had another job after the takeover working in the education field for someone who had been a staunch supporter of Dakota. She had many family members working there also. We received many complaints regarding a couple of them. It was obvious they took advantage of having her as their boss and got away with things that the rest of the staff would not have. I had met with her regarding this problem and other concerns that we had. Rather than face some constructive criticism, on her part, she chose to make my job more difficult. I had gotten called out to fire on a week-end and she fired me while I was gone.

More recently, I have moved to the eastern end of the Upper Peninsula. The various types of work that I've done since I've been here are substitute teaching, construction clean-up, house cleaning, and I joined the volunteer fire department.

Do you remember, as a youngster in school, how your class treated substitute teachers? Well, things haven't changed much. If anything, some high school students seem even more unruly and disrespectful. I don't have the patience for it. I substituted for a couple of years, grades K-12.

I started going to the fire department meetings as an auxiliary volunteer. There is a great need for firefighters on most departments. Some departments have had to close their doors due to so few volunteers. In the township where I now live, they became aware of my experience in wildland fire. They asked me if I would take the training and become certified. I jumped at the opportunity. It's also fulfilling to be serving my community again. We haven't been called to any house fires since I've been on the department. We stay busy with the training sessions that keep us familiar with the equipment. We have responded to more accidents than fires.

Structure fire-fighting is very different from wildland fires. The training took almost six months to complete. I find it to be so interesting and didn't realize the many factors first responders have to consider in their job.

I still do construction clean-up for the same company as when I lived in Republic, MI. It is part-time and on an "as needed" basis. Their work area encompasses the central and eastern U.P.

I do a little house cleaning on the side. The couple I work for have a beautiful, big house, by a lake. They also own a construction company and hire me to do extra work, now and then, regarding clean-up.

I'm feeling more settled in my life now, finally. I thought this might be the ideal time to sit at the computer to reflect and share my story. As I recall these memories, I shake my head in disbelief, amazed that I am still here.

I've heard criticism from some, "All of that education, what did that get her? She didn't exactly set the world on fire now, did she? What a waste." Well, I don't start fires. I put them out. There will always be criticism out there to face. Just because I didn't land a job in my field of study does not mean that I've lost all of that accumulated knowledge. My education has given me a richer life.

I have applied for many jobs, in this area, for positions where I know I was qualified. When they find out that I do not have managerial experience they are not willing to give me a chance to get the experience. I realize our country has federal laws that protect against age discrimination, but I believe it still occurs. It is difficult to prove. It seems as though employers prefer younger college graduates that are more computer tech savvy. I'm not ready to apply as a greeter at Walmart just yet.

I enjoy watching the surprised look on people's faces when they make assumptions about me but don't really have a clue. I've talked about certain jobs I felt qualified to apply for and have been asked, "Oh, do you have a degree?" I think all they see is an Indian in worn out jeans, tennis shoes, and t-shirt. "Yea, a couple of them," I gleefully respond.

Perhaps my writing is what I was meant to do. As for the critics, you know what they say, "you can please some of the people some of the time but you can't please all of the people all of the time." This book has been therapeutic for me and if it touches just one person in a special way then it is well worth it.

OLD FIRE DOG

In 1996, my cousin, the one in the same who ate the yuckies for us at Harbor Springs, lived next door to us in Watersmeet, and was thick as thieves with my brother Luther, told me about the wildland firefighting job he had. He and some other young guys from the reservation had been doing it for a number of years and making some good money. They had just gotten back from a detail out west and were sitting around his apartment talking about it.

I was spellbound listening to their experiences of traveling to different parts of the country, camping, hiking the mountains, the dangers of fighting forest fires, and the rewarding feeling when the townspeople expressed their gratitude to them. He said, almost embarrassingly, that the public treated them like they were heroes. Everywhere they went people held up signs that read, "Thank You, Firefighters." People were coming up to them wanting to shake their hands and telling them, "God bless you." He said the work was hard but if a person were in shape, he could handle it. He knew they were looking for more people and encouraged me to apply.

I started to seriously consider doing it and wondered what other females I could persuade to join. My other cousin, his sister, and a friend of mine that I had gotten close to during the takeover, expressed an interest, also. The three of us decided to take the class together. They rode with me, and we drove the hour-long trip to Watersmeet for the weeklong training sponsored by the Ottawa Forest Service.

Although this was a male-dominated field, we were not intimidated. We were all tomboys, not prissy, sissy girls. We weren't afraid to break a nail or get dirty. Our lives prepared us for a life of adventure and taught us how to be one with nature. The three of us were strong Indian women. We were excited to take on the challenge. One of the first warnings our instructor told the class was that it was not going to be a "cake walk." He said that we would not have hot water, electricity, comfortable sleeping arrangements, meals were slow to come at times, and the work would be dirty and grueling." We just looked at each other and whispered, "kind of sounds like home!"

Our weeklong training began with the basics of our necessary gear and tools. It then became more intense and in-depth covering weather behavior, fuels, terrain, map reading, pumps, hoses, safety issues, operational procedures, and other expectations of assignments.

Our gear included: personal protection equipment (PPE), hardhat with shroud, nomex (fire-resistant shirt and pants), leather boots, leather gloves, earplugs, safety glasses, daypack (for carrying lunch, water, flares, headlamp, batteries), and of course, most importantly, our fire shelter (which was only to be used in the event of a burnover). It was deployed by taking it out of the container, shaken out, then crawled into face down and spread eagle, and held down with your hands and feet. It resembled a pup-tent.

The hand tools we would be using to construct our firelines included: the pulaski (combination axe head and flatter curved cutter for grubbing, cutting roots), combi-tool (small shovel and pick for scraping and digging), McCloud (combination rake and hoe), and naturally, a shovel (digging and scraping).

Additional equipment used were chainsaws and the dreaded bladderbags. I say dreaded because it is a collapsible bag that holds about five gallons of water with an attached hose. Therefore, in addition to the weight one carries, when this backpack is put on over your daypack, it is about 35-40 more pounds. When climbing steep terrain or traversing over rough footpaths, it becomes difficult and uses up much of your energy. Women are treated no differently and perform the same duties as the men. We also brought flares and driptorches for backfires.

The western states had wildfires every year. Our training, however, couldn't prepare us for the elevation of the mountainous terrain, the extreme heat, the cold nights, the long days, heavy smoke, falling trees and rolling rocks, or the dangerous critters we would be exposed to. Other hazards to be mindful of were mountain lions, scorpions, poisonous snakes and spiders, poison ivy, poison oak, to name a few.

My very first fire was in Bailey, CO. We were at an altitude of 8,500 feet. Being the "flatlanders," that we were, we could only walk a few feet before you had to stop and catch your breath. Walking slowly on the sides of my feet, side-sloping to get to a hot spot, I dared not look down. It was not uncommon for some to find out that they had a mild case of acrophobia (fear of heights). It was such a long distance to the bottom and at times there was nothing to grab on to if you did slip. There were small pebbles that felt as though I was walking on marbles. For those who became fearful, you also experienced vertigo, and your sense of balance had a spinning sensation. I was asking myself, "What was I thinking? What did I get myself into?" Most of us experienced the symptoms of altitude sickness, such as headaches, dizziness, nausea, and shortness of breath. It took a few days to become acclimated.

I loved to walk and hike, but the three to five mile hikes in, just to get to your assigned division of the fire, was not much fun to take back out after a 12-14-hour shift. The hike wasn't only long but involved high stepping over rocks and logs, stooping, jumping, crawling, etc. Some days felt like every muscle and bone on you was sore, bruised, calloused, or swollen.

I found out what getting "bitch-slapped" was when following too close behind the person in front of me. He moved the branch out of his way, walked through, and when it came back, it hit me in the face. The only energy left at the day's end was spent eating a late meal and then flopping into my sleeping bag. We were in shape when we returned home, though. I was so euphoric that I felt like I could have ran a marathon.

Each fire detail was different. Sometimes we were put up in cabins, sometimes in motels, mats on the floor at an armory or school, lawns, fields, tents, and even right on the ground in sleeping bags. The base camp was the location where the fire was managed. It consisted of overhead from the multi-agencies involved such as planning, operations, finance, medical, etc. Also on scene were the crews, equipment, private contractors for meals, porta-johns, showers, laundry etc. Sometimes the fire camps were small while other incidents resembled a "tent city," depending on the size of the fire.

When we came in from a nightshift and approached fire camp, it looked as though you were driving into some small town. Lights lit up the perimeter of the encampment. The noise level, at times, made it difficult to talk over and could be heard from a distance. The sound of generators running and heavy equipment entering and leaving was continuous. The incidents are operated in a para-military style, making them well coordinated and efficiently managed. It has a tiered chain-of-command from the Incident commander (IC) at the top down, to smoke jumpers, hotshot crews, engine crews, and handcrews at the bottom. The handcrew chain-of–command went from the crewboss, squad bosses, then the firefighters.

Most National Forests fires out west ranged from 50,000 to 100,000 acres, some were larger, and some were smaller. The causes varied from lightning strikes to arson. I have had the opportunity to work on fires in Oregon, California, Idaho, Montana, Nevada, Arizona, Texas, Utah, and Colorado, all beautiful states with their rugged terrain and snow-capped, or rocky mountains. Our tribal fire crew has also worked closer to home in Minnesota, Wisconsin, Ohio, and our own home state of Michigan.

For the first few years, our tribal members went out on fire with the Ottawa National Forest crew, whose main office was in Watersmeet. At that time, the crews' details were obligated for three weeks. Nationally, it was determined that many of the firefighter injuries occurred during the last week. So, the details were shortened to two weeks, not including travel time.

As we gained experience, we observed that we seemed to be getting the "short end of the stick." We did not get equal opportunity for training or calls to fire. Not only was our pay inferior but so was our equipment or gear. We were paid half the wage of what forest service employees were getting, for doing the same work, and we did not earn overtime wages. Sometimes we waited months to get paid. When the opportunity presented itself, Keweenaw Bay had built up enough experience to start a new crew.

Through the hard work of some individuals, networking with other tribes, and a little patience and persistence, the Keweenaw Bay Tribe created the only tribal wildland fire crew east of the Mississippi. With assistance from the Bureau of Indian Affairs, the "Beartown Firefighters," newly named, established national recognition as a Type II Fire crew. Beartown has since expanded their fire program with a cache, rigs, firefighter trainings, and perform public education and fire prevention duties. They are a mobile, independent resource that is available to be dispatched to incidents at the national level.

Generally, a 20-man crew assists other governmental agencies such as the Forest Service, Department of Natural Resources, Fish & Wildlife, Parks & Recreation, as well as local fire departments. Fire crews also get dispatched to other natural disasters in addition to wildfires. For example, Beartown has helped out with an ice storm in Ohio and worked with FEMA after Hurricane Katrina devastated the Panhandle.

FEMA directed us to do the inventory of the travel trailers that were going to be used as temporary housing for victims of the disaster. We were staying in Texarkana, Arkansas at a local motel. Displaced residents from the hurricane were traveling through the area. After hours, we sat in the dining area of the motel, and listened to horror stories from some of the survivors.

An elderly, Black gentleman told us that he and a friend of his had waded through water up to their hips. They were trying to get back to their house to see what they could salvage. All of sudden, his friend disappeared right next to him. An alligator had came by, snatched him and took the man under. He sat in his chair, with his paper bag of worldly possessions, clutching a rotten banana, as if it were his last meal. The glazed-over look, and far-away stare in his eyes, relayed the shock of what he had just been through. Our hearts went out to him.

We have seen other homeless victims out in California. Our mode of transportation was mostly school busses. We were on our way to the fire and going through a busy part of a town. As we pulled up to a red light at the intersection, homeless people held up signs saying, "Will work for Food." This was a scene, up until then, that we had only seen in the movies. They also had desperation in their eyes as they stood there begging on the street corners. We had just got done eating at a fast-food restaurant. In the back of the bus, we had a box of prepared lunches for our shift. We had someone jump out of the bus and give them the food. They were so happy and wouldn't stop thanking us. Everyone got quiet on the bus, feeling sad about what we had just witnessed. We realized that, yes, we didn't have much back home, but these people had absolutely nothing but the clothes on their backs. "I feel good that we did that," one of the younger firefighters said. I know we have homeless people in the Upper Peninsula, but you don't see them standing on the street corners holding up signs. Usually some family member will take them in.

The fascinating sights we got to enjoy out west were the mountains, the ocean, the Redwoods, the desert, and the Golden Gate Bridge. The Golden Gate Bridge, for all that you hear about it, doesn't have anything over on our local, mighty, Mackinaw Bridge. It is small in comparison and not as well maintained. California, with its larger population, also has a high crime rate, something we don't have to be too concerned about. When we arrived at the Los Angeles Airport, we witnessed a mugging right in the parking lot. Some woman was screaming and two security guards were chasing the culprit. If we were to see someone running away from a crime scene back home, chances are, you probably know who they are.

We were dispatched to the Boundary Waters in northern Minnesota. It was a series of islands and designated wilderness area. Some of the islands were burning. We would be canoeing for the entire detail. Remember that I can't swim a stroke, and I float like a rock. I was a little fearful and kept reminding everyone to grab me if our canoe tipped over or if I happened to go under.

It was quite the adventure! We were flown close to the designation on a beaver, or floatplane, with our canoes attached to the plane. It was about a 6-hour trek of paddling and portaging. I thought my arms were going to fall off. We paired up and took turns carrying the 70-pound canoes on our backs over the portages. The partner carried all of the gear (packs and tools), which was equally as heavy. They choppered in our food and dropped it off in a sling net.

One day as we worked the hot spots, we came upon smoke drifting up from where an outhouse had burned up. There was a hole in the ground about 6' by 8'. Two of our guys had to jump down in there and literally stir the shit. As I recall, it was two greenhorns. We set up our pumps near the lake and ran hoses to the hotspots. So we sprayed, and they stirred. It splattered up and splashed onto their faces. They were gagging, puking and cursing. All the rest of us could do was laugh our asses off.

We came across wolf tracks, coyote dung, and moose tracks. A mother moose and her calf were spotted on one of the islands. It came over the radio, "There's a moose on the loose," and we had to clear out of the area. The mother was all riled up from all the activity and feeling protective of her calf.

Two of us women paddled back to the campsite an hour earlier than the rest to start cooking up the grub for supper. We had to get a campfire going on the makeshift fire pit first. Sometimes it was hard to get our canoe to go in the direction that we wanted because of the wind. When we left the island, we paddeled and paddeled, and didn't seem to be moving. The wind then took our canoe and blew us back to the shore, in reverse. The guys were holding their stomachs and laughing at us. A few times you could watch couples in their canoe make a circle to the right and then another circle to the left before it would straighten out. You'd never know it was a bunch of Indians out there.

Anyway, one of the food packs had mixings for chocolate pie. We had a large tarp tied over the area where we had the boxed up food, cooking utensils, and our fire pit. Sometimes the smoke would roll through there so thick it burned your eyes. We made our pies and set them on a couple of stumps to cool down before being served as dessert.

The crew got back and lined up to get their helpings. You either sat on the ground or a log to eat. My nephew, one of my sister's boys, happened to be on this fire with us. He was considered a "greenhorn." He had his plate in his hand and was looking for a place to sit down and eat. The smoke was thick as it billowed through under the tarp, making it hard to see. He could barely make out a stump and plopped down on it to eat. He sat right on top of one of our pies! He said that he thought he felt something squishy, stood up, and the chocolate pie was stuck to his ass. He peeled it off but didn't want to tell us what he had done. It looked like he crapped his pants.

We had one other pie to serve. We were in hysterics as we told the guys what had happened. One of the guys had a bite half-way up to his mouth and then stopped as he heard us. "What? You didn't even tell us before we ate it," he asked. We told him it wasn't the pie that he was eating. I was holding the pie with the ass-cheek marks in it as I wondered what to do with it.

One of the younger ones, who was quite the prankster, sauntered up nonchalantly. Not wanting to interrupt the conversation, he looked at the pie, took two fingers and swiped them through the pie, then licked his fingers. "There ain't nothin' wrong with that pie," he stated. We burst out laughing again. He was known to eat all kinds of bugs on a dare. One time they double-dog dared him to eat some gross looking beetle. They had a pot built up to about $20.00. He was chomping on it and it made a crunching sound like a handful of Doritos. It sent shivers down my spine.

It wasn't all fun and games on the fire details. I recall being on a fire in northern California. We had did a "death march," up and down steep terrain and ended up in a deep ravine, cold-trailing. That is a "seek and destroy," mission. As you patrol, you look for hot spots, or small smokes, then work them, with the tools and water until they are cold. We were taking a break in the shade near a creek. Someone happened to look up and seen a big log, still flaming, come hurling down towards us. He screamed our crew boss's name, "watch out, log!" Our crew boss didn't even look to see what was coming. He just dove over the log he was leaning against, headfirst. It was about a 6' drop on the other side of the log. The log that was tumbling down hit the log he was leaning on and caught the top of his backpack as he dove. It hit, took a bounce, and ricocheted in the direction of six of us standing there gasping in horror. Three people jumped in one direction and the other three jumped in the opposite direction. The log flew right in between us. We couldn't believe how close we came to someone getting seriously injured. Our training came in to play. We were taught to look up, look down, look all around, and have situational awareness. We all had to watch out for each other.

We were on another fire, high in the mountains, and it was mid-afternoon. We sat down to take a break in the sweltering heat. We had just completed a progressive hose lay of 1000' down the mountainside. I walked over to the other side of the hill to check out the view. I spotted heavy smoke and flames headed in our direction. I went and asked our crew boss to come and check it out because it seemed to be traveling fast. He quickly gathered up our troops and told us that we needed to hustle it out of the area and get to our designated safety zone. We were still catching our breath from the work we had just gotten done. The safety zone was quite a distance and uphill. Our adrenaline kicked in as it came over our radios, transmitting what we already knew. The fire changed direction and was headed our way, at a good rate of speed. Most of the younger guys made good time. Another girl, a lot younger, but heavier and slower than me, and myself, were at the end of the line.

Our squad bosses and crew boss waited for us, telling us to hurry. I moved as fast as I could, but it felt like I was going in slow motion, as I gasped for air with each step. The girl behind me grabbed herself by her pantlegs, pulling them forward with each step, trying to get her legs to move faster. Our nomex cargo pants had large pockets on the side and she pulled one pocket right off her pant leg.

We kept looking behind to see how close it was getting to us. By then, most of the crew had made it to the top, and we still had a little ways to go. "Come on, come on, hurry!" they were yelling to us. We glanced back and could see the fire burning the area we had just been working. It burned up all of the brand new hose we had just laid and was gaining ground a shorter distance behind us. Thoughts were swirling in my head that she and I were going to have to deploy our fire shelters because I didn't know if we could finish making it up the hill in time. Our squad bosses and crew boss told us that they would have carried us up that hill if they had to. "We leave no man behind," they told us We had made it to our safety zone and watched the fire burn past us.

On another fire out west, one of my cousins from Watersmeet had found and ate a scorpion. Crewmembers were talking about how he cut the tail off and sucked down the rest of it. He said it gave him a quick boost of energy to get up the mountain. We were taking another break once, sitting on a trail in some gravel. Someone looked down and spotted a scorpion. We all started looking down in the rocks and could see we were sitting in a nest of scorpions. Everyone jumped up and moved out of there. A couple of the guys captured two scorpions and put them in an empty water bottle. They wanted to watch them fight.

They came upon a rattlesnake also, during a break. One guy went to take a leak and just about stepped on a rattler. They chopped it up with their Pulaski. That reminded me of my brothers dicing up garter snakes with the axe when we were little. One of the guys kept the rattle off of the snake. I learned then that you could tell how old the snake was by how many rattles it had. This snake had 5 rattles, so it was about 5 years old.

We went on a little tour out west one day and drove around the mighty Redwoods. We also went through a couple of towns that claimed to be home to Bigfoot. We checked out the small museum that told stories and history of the elusive creature. Finding Bigfoot is one of my favorite shows at home today. I don't know of anyone who has seen one though.

One assignment we had was in such a desolate and rugged area, that we had to be choppered in. They gave us a quick briefing on the correct way to enter and exit the chopper. We had to be in full gear, except for our pack, safety glasses on, ear plugs in, shirt buttoned up to the neck and tucked in, sleeves down, gloves on, and walk in a crouched position on and off. They flew us, 6 at a time, in a Blackhawk helicopter. The pilot banked it to the right, then banked it to the left, as we passed through ravines, and in between mountainsides, checking out the fire from above. It was awesome and freaky at the same time. What an experience! It kind of felt like a carnival ride. We were all thrilled and excited about that once-in-a-lifetime experience.

Handcrews usually cleared a helipad for the chopper to land. They did not allow immediate family members to be on the same flight, just in case something happened. If it were to go down, bad enough that a family might lose one member, but to lose more would be too much to bear.

We had a detail where a fatal helicopter crash happened. It killed all the fire personnel on board. The chopper had landed upside down in a creek, then broke into pieces. They had it cordoned off, as they investigated it, but we had to drive by the accident site everyday on our way to work. It was a somber and quiet bus ride as we rode past. It makes you think, "But for the grace of God, that could have been us."

Our crew met so many new people from other fire crews. Many of these crews were Native also, but from western tribes. As we walked past them, we could not understand what they were saying, because they spoke in their own native tongue. They had the same look of pride as we had, on their faces, knowing they were doing their part in helping to protect Aki Mama Nong, Mother Earth. They all thought we were from Canada, with our "yooper" accent. True, we are only a few hours away from the Canadian border, hence the influence, ay?

My cousin, my friend, and I met an interesting fellow while on a fire. He was from New York. He was of Puerto Rican descent. He had a unique ability to look at your hands and tell you things about yourself that there was no possible way he could have known. He was a complete stranger to us. His name was Jose R. He told my cousin and I, after observing our hands, about our grandma Brunk. Jose described her to the letter, the kind of dress she wore with an apron, how she liked to chew tobacco, and wore her grey hair pulled back in a bun. He also told us that in our time of need, she had been there for us, when we were at our lowest point. Many bad things had happened to my cousin too. He had also attended the Harbor Springs School. Funny, I had thought that grandma didn't like her grandchildren, always chasing us away. Now I know why I had left the dock that day.

Everywhere we went, the townspeople were so grateful to us. They treated us as though we were royalty. There were signs posted everywhere, in windows and on marquees, that read, "Thank you Firefighters, Thank You for Saving Our Town!" It was just like my cousin had described when he first related his firefighting experiences.

One of our basecamps was in Mormon country out in Utah. We camped in a basin that was surrounded by mountains. The fairgrounds were right next to our camp. We pitched our tents in the dark upon arrival. We were awoken early the next morning to the sounds of mooing. As we peered out, we were greeted by cows standing there looking at us. We ate well there when we came in off our shift. No MRE's (meals-ready-to-eat) for us. Some of the MRE's were quite gross. I think they were rations left over from the Viet Nam War. They could make a tird but that was about it. The Mormon women cooked up thick steaks that covered our whole plate, corn on the cob, real potatoes, and cake. What a feast that was. Sometimes we ate better than at home and came back a few pounds heavier.

Every day, first thing in the morning, as the sun was coming up, the smoke was heavy and pungent as it hung in the air from the thermal layer. The mornings were usually cold, as we made ourselves get out of the sleeping bags to get geared up. Our task before leaving, was to make sure that you had everything you needed for the day, lunch, water, toilet paper, etc. We marched in single-file directly toward the path of the fire. We were usually warmed up and peeling off jackets by the time we stopped for a quick break and drink of water. We were still bone-weary from the long day before, a restless night's sleep from lying on the ground, and a little stressed from not knowing how the weather would change the fire's behavior. It took at least a few days before the stiffness wore off.

The elements were extreme, the work was hard and dirty, the temperatures were so hot (sometimes-triple digits) during the day and cold at night (sometimes down into the '30's). We've had to hustle down off the mountain ridge during severe thunderstorms. Sometimes there would be no trees or cover and we would huddle together. Hail made a pelting sound as it bounced off of our hardhats.

The fire itself was a force to be reckoned with. We could hear it coming, roaring like a freight train, as it raced up the mountain. When we had to stand there and hold the line, the heat was so intense it felt like you were in an oven. It felt like your skin was going to fall right off as it passed by you. We stood about 10 feet apart from each other, guarding the fireline so it wouldn't slop over into the green. The smoke became so dense that you could not see the people on either side. Your eyes burned and watered, your chest and lungs became tight, as we choked on the smoke waiting for the air to clear.

As the years went by, the more experience we gained, the more effective we became, working as a team. If there was a water supply shortage, we did helmet brigades from the nearest water source. At times, these water sources were not clean, but the hardhats still went right back on our heads. It was not the most sanitary of conditions. Most of the time, our hands were black from the ash, but we ate our sandwiches anyway. It wasn't only our hands, our faces were also black, all dressed in the same gear, it was hard to tell who was who. Sometimes, if we were spiked out, we would not get a shower for days. When a crew is "spiked out," they are far away from base camp and there isn't any portable water, porta-johns, food catering, laundry, etc. It is in desolate country and a chopper, as in the Boundary Waters of Minnesota, slings the food in.

When we are in the bush, we had to walk out of sight to go to the bathroom, and take our tool with us. A hole was dug, you did your thing, and then it was buried. It was very inconvenient for females if we were having our monthly visitor. I always worried that some wild animal would smell it, dig it up, tear it up, and drag it out in plain sight for the whole crew to see. I would have been mortified, but thankfully, that never happened.

One of our bus drivers hung air fresheners all over the bus. We were all smelly, reeking from BO, and filthy from dirt, mud and ash, as we filed onto the bus. Often, we only had 2 sets of nomex to wear for the entire 2 weeks. We would have to put on the same dirty clothes day after day. To clarify, we did have clean underwear and T-shirts under the nomex.

There were times that we had to make a human chain. If the terrain was too steep, we lined out, joined hands, and pulled people up from down below. Usually, it was the sawyers who had the additional weight of their saw, which made climbing cumbersome. Just being a part of that effort strengthened our group cohesiveness. We were all equals out on the fireline. That was our family away from home. The guys treated the women as if we were their sisters, and they acted as if they were our brothers. If it weren't for the extreme heat, cold, danger from fire, fear of falling off a mountain, wild animals, unsanitary conditions, and intense work, it would be just like going camping. You either loved it or you hated it. It is certainly not for everyone.

We usually gave up our summers to go work out west. We missed out on the big 4th of July celebrations and annual pow-wow back home. When we did return home and our loved ones wanted to go camping, they heard a resounding "NO!" All we wanted to do was to sleep in our own nice, soft bed. It didn't take long to nod off upon returning home.

Some potential volunteers quit in the training phase after finding out what they would be in for. Some went out for one fire and never came back. I think there have even been occasions that people have up and walked off from a fire due to the extremes. Your body gets a little beaten up from limbs sticking out, tripping, or hitting yourself with your tool. Sometimes I would come home with many bruises up and down my legs and arms. It looked like someone kicked the shit out of me. You blow black boogers out of your nose for about a week.

One time we were on our way home, and we had to stop in Duluth, MN to spend a night at the armory. I took a shower that night before hitting the rack. I also took one when I got up the next day. When I finally got home later that night, I took a nice leisurely soak in the bathtub before going to bed. When I got out of the tub, there was still a big, black ring all the way around the tub.

Sometimes your feet really paid the price from all of the walking, hiking, and climbing. At the end of the day it would be hard to get your work boots off because your feet would swell. Most of us would compare blisters and callouses on our toes, heels, and soles of our feet. God forbid, if you had to break in a pair of new boots on the fire. This happened to quite a few greenhorns, with much regret. I've seen some peeling off bloody socks. They painfully limped around and were told to "suck it up."

One fire, someone had actually forgotten to bring his fire boots. We had the chartered bus stop at a nearby Walmart, so he could buy another pair. We got going down the road to the fire. He opened his shoebox and discovered that there were two left boots in the box. How does that happen? It was funny but an inconvenience to the crew. He ended getting another pair before we got there.

The most memorable story about my wildland firefighting career happened on our own turf. Newberry, MI is located towards the eastern end of the U.P. Up until then, we were treated very well around the country, except for Texas. (They were not as friendly towards us. It was almost as if they still held resentment for losing the war. Everything is bigger in Texas, especially the attitudes.) It took a wild fire in our own back yard to help us remember and appreciate what we have here at home. Our small, rural land that lacks so much, compared to bustling, urban areas, but the beauty, clean air, fresh water, and kindness from people is the trade-off.

The traffic on our radios transmitted the same "yooper," accent that we had. The elderly ladies that volunteered for the American Red Cross and the Salvation Army had set up a small store stocked with food and supplies for the firefighters. We often had commissary tents on large fires out west, but they did not have the type of "goodies," that were here. Free for the taking, they told us to grab a bag and take whatever we wanted. There were pop, snacks, doughnuts, toiletries, brand new T-shirts, underwear, and socks still in the package, and many other needed articles. Most, if not all, of our crew came from low-income families. The young guys threw away their raggedy, old T-shirts they had brought and filled their bags with new articles. They were astonished that everything was free. They came out smiling from ear-to-ear, as if they had just won a shopping spree at Walmart.

There was a prison that was located in this town. We had heard that the operation had the prisoners making the lunches for the crews. I noticed that some of the guys were not eating their lunch. When I asked why they were not eating they said that they knew the prisoners made the sandwiches. I didn't understand the connection. They said, "Well, prisoners have so much time on their hands that they have nothing better to do than to screw with the food for amusement." "What do you mean?" I asked. They replied, "Do you really think that's mayonnaise on your sandwich?" Enough said. After that, most of the crew quit eating lunch and were "starvin' marvins," by the time we came in for dinner.

We had busted our butts all day, trying to get the fire contained, and were coming back into town after our shift. They actually gave us a police escort to and from the fire area. There was a long convoy of heavy equipment, firetrucks, engines, school busses with the fire crews, and ambulances standing by. We looked out our windows to see the streets lined with people on both sides. They were cheering, clapping, and holding up signs. "Something's going on, looks like a parade," someone on the bus said. "We're the parade," someone else said, as they read "Thank You Firefighters," on the signs. All of a sudden it got real quiet on the bus. No one said a word. I couldn't even look at anyone. I knew everyone else was as choked up as I was and had tears in their eyes. We felt it was unnecessary to thank us for doing our job. To be respected and acknowledged in such a manner was exalting. It was very rewarding to be part of something that was making a real difference. The applause was for the Department of Natural Resources, the Forest Service, Volunteer Fire Departments, and all other resources involved that worked so diligently.

That good feeling happened one other time on a fire down near the Ohio/ Kentucky border. The incident commander had rounded us up for a briefing after an exhaustive day. "We covered a lot of ground, put in some hard work, and contained the fire. You should feel very proud. Today, you saved lives, property, and this town," he told us. Tears silently rolled down my cheeks, and I wanted to burst out and cry like a baby.

I flashed back to my mother leaving and us crying, the nuns, the many nights of crying myself to sleep, the years of sexual abuse, my leaving and my children crying, my failed marriages, and me sitting on the edge of that dock. That pat on the back negated those hurtful memories.

One of the most challenging climbs on a fire detail was out west, but I don't remember which state. It could have been California or Idaho. It had some of the steepest terrain we ever had to deal with. We climbed that mountain for six or seven hours straight. We literally had to use our tools to pull ourselves upward. We were crawling on our stomachs. Every time we got to, what we thought was the top, we looked up only to see another summit to climb. We literally had our heads in the clouds. I thought we were about to see God. One of the guys did not have his chin-strap on. His helmet fell off and tumbled down the mountain quite far. Luckily, someone down below grabbed it, before he was doomed to spend a couple of hours retrieving it.

I was the only female on a squad sent downstate for a detail. One of the squad bosses said, "Oh great, a female in the rig, now I suppose we're going to have to watch our language!" I said "Ya, you don't want to sound like a greenhorn." One morning, listening to the news in the truck, we heard that a cop had been arrested for harassment of a female he had pulled over. It was a bizarre story of how he had "licked her hair." "He must have been licking her pubic hair," I said. "Ewe, gross, Linda," they said in disgust. "What? I'm just trying to speak your lingo," I told them. They laughed because they knew I had the same sick sense of humor they had. I had been around enough jailbirds, construction workers, perverts, and guys with one-track minds, to know how they think. I would make them blush before they would me.

I was the second, oldest person on the crew, and my body felt it. I was proud to have worked with them. I miss those times and think of them often. We old firedogs are being replaced with much younger greenhorns. They are learning from the best. It is good to see. It is also good to see that the young females are not being intimidated by work that is in a male-dominated field. The Beartown Firefighters are still going out and kicking ash.

REFLECTIONS

When I see my reflection in the mirror looking back at me, it scares me... not really. I know I'm still a head-turner. Only now they turn the other way when they see me coming...not really. But seriously, I do see a face etched from the many expressions over the years as I have lived, laughed, and loved. All of my trials and tribulations have made me stronger and have culminated into the person I am today. I've survived trauma, faced disappointments, and dealt with the pain that comes with life.

If my time to leave this world should come tomorrow, I will go out knowing that I have lived a full life. I did everything I wanted, accomplished my feats, have been to places I never thought I would, and had meaning in my life. In my youth, I didn't think I would get out of the U.P. I yearned to see the mountains and the ocean. I wanted to do something that meant something. I wanted to, somehow, give something back to my community and my country. I have completed my bucket list.

Although, three of my marriages ended in divorced, I have no regrets. My first husband gave me four of the most beautiful children in the world. I can't help thinking that it took my leaving for him to become the great father to them that he remains to be today. We both finally matured enough to be able to get along and are civil to each other. Together, we are the proud grandparents to our 16, and counting, grandchildren.

My short, second marriage gave me a glimpse of how "the other half," lives. I now know that I am not a "city," girl. I fit better in the country, specifically, the Upper Peninsula. I felt what it was like to be put up on a pedestal and then spoiled rotten. That wasn't me either. I must say, it boosted my self-esteem, and it felt good for awhile. Maybe I thought I didn't deserve it because there are plenty who deserve it, but don't get it. Who am I? I'm no better than they are. Maybe I thought nothing good ever lasts long in my life, so, I'll leave before I am left again.

In my last marriage, I gained the confidence to stand up for others and myself. As I watched my partner fight for what he believed in, I was able to see what bravery and courage can accomplish. We just started to slide backwards to a place I did not want to be again, in poverty.

The abandonment by my parents and the sexual abuse issues became my biggest fight in life. The PTSD takes over and there is no stopping it. I will continue that search for love.

Yes, there were three divorces, but no, I have never asked for anything from them. I did not want a house, spousal support, car, nothing, except for my clothes and personal belongings, such as pictures. The gossips liked to tell of how I took everything I could get. They also enjoy thinking that I just left my kids. No, that is what happened to me.

As for my job-hopping, I liked the variety, the experiences, the knowledge gained, and the friends I made, while taking temporary positions. It made my life more well-rounded.

I married for the fourth time, incredulously. We have been together for 9 years. He knows all about my baggage. I think we all have issues of some sort that we bring into our relationships. He is hard working, loving, and his quiet demeanor has a calming effect on me. We take good care of each other. He has no children but helped raise two with his ex. We have a nice place, out in the woods, where it is quiet and conducive to writing.

My hubby doesn't always "get" my sense of humor. He is not the only one. My Native brothers and sisters "get it" though. It is something our people have used in order to cope with the historical trauma we have lived through. I have only recently been studying the theory of "historical trauma," that I ran across on the Internet while writing my book. It makes sense and I believe it to be true. It purports that the cause of today's health crisis, among Native Americans, was shaped by the U.S. federal policies. It goes on to state that the historical losses of our population, land, and culture has left a legacy of chronic trauma and unresolved grief across generations. If I am to write another book, I wish to delve into this aspect further and look at how it correlates to the boarding school experience.

On a lighter note, I have found my greatest contribution to leaving this world in a little better place was bringing my four children into it. They have been my greatest blessing from the Creator. What a marvel that something so beautiful can come from another beautiful act. The pain from the four caesarian sections was quickly forgotten the minute I heard their first wails.

Admittedly, I see the genes of their father in all of them, from their looks, to their bone structure, mannerisms, humor, kindness, and their character. By the same token, I see myself in them, from their big, round dark eyes, to their silly sense of humor, their humbleness, their compassion for their fellow mankind, their strength, and zest for life.

They far surpass what it means to be a good parent and spouse than what their father and I modeled for them. My kids are loyal, dedicated, and very loving toward their families. They enjoy being parents that are actively involved in the grandchildren's education by homeschooling. They have strong religious values and provide a comfortable living for their families.

I love all of my children and would give my life for any of them. They had a very hard life growing up. Similar to their dad and me, they went without, and often. They never asked for anything, nor did they complain about what they did not have. They are humble in spirit, never arrogant. They are kind and respectful of people.

At times when they were younger, there was little to eat. We lived on commodities, and had an income at the poverty level. They didn't have the luxuries of running water and a toilet for some time. We could not afford to give them much materialistically. They came from a broken family. I'm sure they were tortured at school from other kids who did have all of those things.

166

In spite of all of that, they still had more than their father and I had. Their parents always loved them. They have brought us so much joy and happiness. All we can do is keep trying to make up for what we didn't give them, what they never had, but what they deserve.

We do the best we can, given where we come from. Sometimes we don't understand ourselves how or why we make the decisions that we do. Some things you can be sure of in life. You will experience pain and you will make mistakes. But don't let that stop you from trying, taking a risk, or loving. Find the humor in life. It makes life more bearable. If life hands you lemons, squirt someone in the eye with them.

In many ways, I am taking a big risk writing this book, putting myself out there. People will continue to judge me. I have learned along the way that the biggest gossips have the most to hide in their own lives. That is why they keep the conversation going about other people, they don't want to discuss what they've done in their past.

Hopefully, the readers will enjoy my story, and I will sell enough books to be able to pay off my student loan. Have you ever noticed how the student loan people can find you no matter how many times you move, what little arm-pit of the world you move to, they are still able to track you down. It's as if you were on the top ten "most wanted," list.

Home really is where the heart is. I love my house where my husband and I live but by coming back to my tribe, Lac Vieux Desert, in Watersmeet, MI, I was able to find that missing link.

In closing, I find it funny as I contemplate, that "coming full circle," can also mean looking like we did when we were born. We all come into this world bald, with no teeth, a wrinkled, shriveled up little thing, wearing diapers, and then end up going out looking the same way. To age gracefully, we must accept the fact that we will lose our hair, teeth, become wrinkled, and even end up wearing adult diapers. Ain't life grand?!

From left in back; Dad, unknown family friend, Mom.
In front; Melvin, Luther and I in Watersmeet.
Notice my big brother antagonizing me by pulling my braid.

In our healthier and younger days, 1989.
From left; Sisters, Mom and me at right.

Dad Frank George Brunk Jr.
U.S Army, died 1987.

Luther Brunk

USMC, died 1981

Melvin Brunk

U.S. Army, died 1984

Beartown Fire Crew

Sleeper Lake Fire – 2007
Newberry, MI
I am third from left in front.

REFERENCES:

1. <u>America's Fascinating Indian Heritage</u>, Reader's Digest Association, c1978.

2. <u>Courage to Heal</u>, Ellen Bass, Laura Davis, 2008.

3. <u>Like A Hurricane,</u> Paul Chaat Smith, Robert Allen Warrior, 1997.

4. <u>L'Anse Sentinel</u>, L'Anse, MI 49946.

5. <u>Northern Express</u>, "Unholy Childhood," Northern Mich. Largest Newsweekly, June, 2008.

6. American Indian Singers: Buddy Red Bow, Floyd Westerman.

7. Wikipedia, The Free Encyclopedia, Florida Keys.

8. Tpcjournal.nbcc.org/Examining the Theory of Historical Trauma Among Native Americans, 2004, Kathleen Brown-Rice.

9. http://hilo.hawaii.edu/academics/hohonu/documents/Vol04x06=romthemelting pot.pdf, by LeAna B. Gloor.

10. Baragarose.tripod.com-Spring 2000.htm.

11. <u>Detroit Free Press</u>, March, 1996, Tina Lam.

12. Indian Country Today Media Network.com, Konnie Lemay, A Brief History of American Indian Military Service.

13. Fireline Handbook, January 1998, NWCG Handbook 3, PMS 410-1, NFES 0065.

14. www.thewildwest.org/component/content/article/28.html.

15. www.sott.net/article/234783, United Truth Seekers, reported by C. Young, 9-8-11.